Taxcafe.co.uk Tax Guides

How to Avoid Stamp Duty

By Russell Eaton

Important Legal Notices:

TAXCafe™
TAX GUIDE - "How to Avoid Stamp Duty"

Published by:
Taxcafe UK Limited
214 High St
Kirkcaldy, KY1 1JT, UK
Tel: (0044) 01592 560081
Email: team@taxcafe.co.uk

Third Edition, April 2005

ISBN 1-904608-22-1

Disclaimer

1. This tax guide is sold subject to the condition that neither the publisher nor the author can be held legally responsible for the consequences of any errors, omissions, or advice given in the book. Please note that this tax guide is intended as general guidance only for individual readers and does NOT constitute legal, accountancy, tax, investment or other professional advice. Taxcafe UK Limited accepts no responsibility or liability for loss which may arise from reliance on information contained in this tax guide.

2. Please note that tax legislation, the law and practices by government and regulatory authorities (e.g. the Inland Revenue) are constantly changing. We therefore recommend that for legal, accountancy, tax, investment or other professional advice, you consult a suitably qualified solicitor, accountant, tax specialist, independent financial adviser, or other professional adviser. Please also note that your personal circumstances may vary from the general examples given in this tax guide and your professional adviser will be able to give specific advice based on your personal circumstances.

3. This tax guide covers UK taxation only and any references to 'tax' or 'taxation' in this guide, unless the contrary is expressly stated, refer to UK taxation only. Please note that references to the 'UK' do not include the Channel Islands or the Isle of Man. Foreign tax implications are beyond the scope of this tax guide.

4. Whilst in an effort to be helpful, this guide may refer to general guidance on matters other than UK taxation, Taxcafe UK Limited is not expert in these matters and does not accept any responsibility or liability for loss which may arise from reliance on such information contained in this tax guide.

5. Please note that Taxcafe UK Limited has relied wholly on the expertise of the author in the preparation of the content of this tax guide. The author is not an employee of Taxcafe UK Limited but has been selected by Taxcafe UK Limited using reasonable care and skill to write the content of this tax guide.

Arrangement of Contents

Read PART ONE if you are *buying* property.

Read PART TWO if you are *selling* property.

Read PARTS ONE & TWO if you are doing both, such as moving house.

PARTS ONE & TWO are written as two separate self-contained books.

PART THREE covers other stamp duty avoidance possibilities, including commercial property

For Property Buyers

Several strategies revealed in this book show exactly how to buy residential or non-residential property without incurring the cost of stamp duty. Each easy-to-follow procedure shows how to make savings amounting to thousands of pounds.

But how, you may ask, can you legally avoid paying stamp duty? Just follow the simple step-by-step strategies in this book and you will never have to find money again to pay for stamp duty.

Some of the strategies in this book are widely used by house-building companies. These companies offer incentives such as a lump sum of cash and 'stamp duty paid' deals when you buy a house. This book shows Buyers how to get these same incentives in any house deal!

Little known, but perfectly legal, trade secrets show how you can get big cash incentives and 'stamp duty paid' deals *whoever* you are buying from. The same strategies used by national building companies have been adapted for use by private individuals buying from other private individuals.

So whether you're a professional buy-to-let investor, a developer, or a private individual buying a home, this book is for you. It shows how to buy a property even if you don't have enough money to pay for stamp duty, legal fees, or a mortgage deposit!

*****

Selling Property – Please see next page

For Property Sellers

Several strategies reveal exactly how to sell residential or non-residential property quickly and profitably. You do this by offering certain financial incentives to potential Buyers. Incentives such as 'stamp duty paid' can go a long way to make your property stand out from the crowd.

Better still, when a potential Buyer wishes to negotiate, this book shows how best to get the full asking price, and bag the sale by use of a powerful and unique strategy.

But how, you say, can a Seller legally offer a 'stamp duty paid' deal without financial loss? Just follow the simple step-by-step strategies in this book and from now onwards you will always want to offer a property free of stamp duty.

Some strategies in this book are widely used by house-building companies, offering incentives such as a lump sum of cash and 'stamp duty paid' deals to potential Buyers. This book shows Sellers exactly how to offer the same incentives in any house deal!

Trade secrets, little known but perfectly legal, show how to offer big cash incentives and 'stamp duty paid' deals *whoever* you may be. These same strategies used by national building companies have been adapted for use by private individuals selling to other private individuals.

So whether you're a professional property investor, a developer, or a private individual selling a home, this book is a must. It shows how to offer an irresistible deal to a potential Buyer, by ensuring a sale at the price you want.

*****

Contents

PART ONE

PROPERTY BUYERS

Introduction

When buying or selling property this book can save you thousands of pounds. When you *buy* a property you will save at least the cost of stamp duty, and when you *sell* you will be able to offer the property free of stamp duty to get a better response (and even a better price). Either way you will win every time.

This book focuses on the buying and selling of property in the UK. PARTS 1 and 2 cover residential property. PART 3 covers other ways of avoiding stamp duty, including land, commercial and non-residential property.

Most of the stamp-duty-avoidance strategies described in this book cannot be used in property auctions unless you can negotiate direct with the Seller, and have the property withdrawn from auction. Basically, the strategies in this book depend on some kind of direct contact between Buyer and Seller, or their estate agents.

Note that in Scotland, property transactions are often *negotiated* through solicitors. Therefore, if you are buying or selling property in Scotland you are urged to make *direct contact with the Buyer or Seller* as applicable. The fact that conveyancing laws in Scotland are different to the rest of the UK should not affect the principles and strategies covered in this book.

You may be wondering how it is possible to *legally* avoid paying stamp duty on property. Clearly, the tax authorities are not going to be deprived of their tax, and this book does not set out to do this. What we are talking about here is a mix of legal avoidance, paying *less*, and making *savings*. For example, you will see how you can pay nil stamp duty on properties up to £150,000, or how you can legally pay £2,000 in stamp duty instead of, say, £5,000. Or you will learn how you can make savings in property transactions that are equal to or greater than the amount of stamp duty. The net result is that you can usually avoid most or all of the cost of stamp duty.

Using these strategies *Sellers* can also benefit by being able to bridge a price gap. For example if an offer to buy falls short by £4,000, the Seller can use the strategies in this book to bridge the £4,000 gap without financial loss, and get the full asking price.

Several powerful stamp-duty-avoidance strategies are explained in this book; a kind of à-la-carte menu of stamp-duty-avoidance strategies. A brief summary is given at the end of each strategy – but please do not be tempted to just read the summaries as you will miss valuable tips and explanations.

In practice you will be using two or three of these strategies whenever dealing in property, providing substantial savings that are usually much more than just the cost of stamp duty. Such strategies are very special and effective, and at least one is likely to work each time you buy or sell a property. If you trade in property professionally such strategies will help to ensure the success of your business.

This book is written as an instruction manual, and as such, it contains step-by-step procedures with easy to follow examples. Some points are repeated for added emphasis and to aid comprehension.

To fully appreciate the savings involved let's look at stamp duty costs. The rates of stamp duty are as shown in fig. 1:

FIG. 1 - RATES OF STAMP DUTY

Property Price	Stamp Duty
Not more than £120,000	0%
More than £120,000 but not more than £250,000	1%
More than £250,000 but not more than £500,000	3%
More than £500,000	4%

This means that on a house worth £200,000 you would pay £2,000 in stamp duty. And as soon as you get up to say £300,000, the stamp duty climbs to £9,000! So clearly stamp duty amounts to thousands of pounds, rather than hundreds, and the amounts are of major significance when considering just about any property transaction.

Stamp duty is short for *'Stamp Duty Land Tax'* and is often abbreviated to SDLT in official documents. In this book we will refer to it simply as 'stamp duty'.

But what exactly is stamp duty? In the context of property or land, stamp duty is nothing more than a property tax. The tax is based on the purchase value of the property.

The tax authorities make no distinction between the property and the fixtures and fittings attached to the property. In other words, fixtures and fittings are also taxable. So if a house is bought for £100,000 and you reckon the fixtures and fittings are worth £3,000, you cannot pay stamp duty on only £97,000. This is discussed in more detail in the chapter *'The Threshold Strategy For Buyers'*.

When a Buyer pays stamp duty, the solicitor passes the money onto the tax authorities together with the address of the property. As a property Buyer, you will find that when you get your solicitor's bill, the stamp duty will be listed along with other disbursements such as valuation fees, legal fees, deposits, money transfer costs, and the like. This cannot be avoided; but the powerful strategies about to be examined will enable you to recover a large part of these costs in ways unknown to the vast majority of home buyers and sellers.

For ease of reference, this publication falls into two parts: *Part One* for people who are BUYING a property. *Part Two* for those SELLING a property. Each part is completely self-contained, as if they were two separate books. Therefore, the reader's forbearance is appreciated where duplication appears.

You need to read both parts when buying *and* selling (which is often the case if you are moving house). Please do not be tempted to skip pages or you may miss important information – study each page carefully and it will repay you handsomely.

Clearly, some aspects of the strategies presented here may not apply to each and every property transaction. However, it is certain that some or many aspects of the strategies *will* apply, particularly if you are buying or selling property and are able to deal directly with the Buyer or Seller (or with an estate agent). Therefore, as you read this book you are bound to discover 'golden nuggets' that best apply to your situation, and you will be able to start using them straight away to save a significant amount of money during your property transactions.

In this book the words 'he/his' are used to include 'she/hers'.

Financial Terms Used

Several financial terms referred to in this book come into play when buying or selling property:

1. **PRICE.** This is the purchase price agreed with the seller and is the figure entered on all the paperwork (including the Land Registry) as the SELLING PRICE. This is also the figure that will be used by the Lender or Mortgage Company to work out how much money to lend. Note that the PRICE does not include PURCHASE COSTS (see below).

2. **PURCHASE COSTS.**

   - These are the additional costs incurred when buying a property, and include legal fees, conveyancing fees, estate agent fees, surveyor costs, valuation costs, council searches, renovation costs, buildings insurance, **stamp duty**, payments for fixtures, fittings, carpets, furniture and the like.

   - Clearly some PURCHASE COSTS may not apply to a particular purchase, but others will always apply, the point being: PURCHASE COSTS cannot normally be included in the loan or mortgage. You have to find the money for PURCHASE COSTS from personal savings or other sources.

3. **LOAN.** This is the amount of money borrowed to buy a property (referred to as the mortgage or loan). The amount of the LOAN is based on the PRICE. For example, a 95% LTV (Loan To Value) means that you get a loan that is equivalent to 95% of the PRICE. The expression *Loan To Value* is used (rather than Loan To Price) because Lenders base the amount of the loan on the valuation that they carry out before giving you the money. Provided that the valuation is not *lower* than the PRICE, you will get a loan based on the PRICE. In the United Kingdom you can typically get LOANS that vary between 70% and 100% of the PRICE. If the LOAN is 100% you will borrow an amount of money equal to the PRICE, and hence not have to pay a deposit.

4. **DEPOSIT.** This is the amount paid towards the PRICE. For example, if you get a 95% LOAN, the deposit is the balance of 5%. Where funds are scarce a person will naturally opt for as big a LOAN as possible, thus minimizing the DEPOSIT.

5. **CONVEYANCING COSTS.** These relate to the legal fees, valuation fees, council searches, stamp duty, and other costs applied by your solicitor or conveyancer.

    Normally, the amount of the LOAN does not take into account any CONVEYANCING COSTS; in other words, you cannot ask the Lender to give you extra money for CONVEYANCING COSTS. The terms LEGAL COSTS and CONVEYANCING COSTS are interchangeable in this book.

Clearly there is an overlap between the PURCHASE COSTS and the CONVEYANCING COSTS in the sense that many of the same costs come under both headings. The point to keep in mind is that some PURCHASE COSTS are not channelled through the solicitor, e.g. you may agree to buy some furniture from the Seller by paying for it directly without involving the solicitor. The stamp duty is shown under two headings: PURCHASE COSTS *and* CONVEYANCING COSTS. Typically, the Buyer will pay the stamp duty to the solicitor (this is not normally included in the LOAN), and the solicitor will pay it on to the Inland Revenue with details of the address. There is no legal way to avoid the payment of stamp duty when a property transaction requires that stamp duty be applied. However, this book shows how this cost can be recovered (or reduced), so that in effect you end up not incurring the cost of stamp duty.

The seven stamp-duty-avoidance-strategies that follow are shown in Fig.2 (on the next page).

FIG. 2 - THE SEVEN STAMP DUTY AVOIDANCE STRATEGIES FOR BUYERS

1	The Tax Exemption Strategy For Buyers
2	The Threshold Strategy For Buyers
3	The Link Strategy For Buyers
4	The Mortgage Cashback Strategy For Buyers
5	The Price Strategy For Buyers
6	The Valuation Strategy For Buyers
7	The Combination Strategy For Buyers

8

The Tax Exemption Strategy For Buyers

In the UK there are hundreds of 'Designated Disadvantaged Areas' (DDAs) spread all over the country, although there are not many in the more affluent shires of South East England. Glasgow for example has many DDAs. The point is this: if a residential property is purchased in a DDA no stamp duty applies if the value is not over £150,000. If the value is over £150,000 the normal rules apply.

Note: Stamp duty rules for commercial property (i.e. non-residential property) are the same, whether located in a DDA or not. In other words, there is no stamp duty relief for commercial property by virtue of being located in a DDA.

It is not, of course, being suggested that you buy a residential property in a DDA in order to escape stamp duty! But it is worth checking whether the property you want to buy is in a DDA. If it is not, this particular strategy cannot be applied. If the property *is* in a DDA, it means that you can buy the property completely free of stamp duty if the value is not over £150,000.

DDAs are also referred to as *Enterprise Areas* because the government wants to encourage economic growth in such areas (hence the stamp duty concession).

To see a list of DDAs (too many to list here) go to:
http://www.inlandrevenue.gov.uk/so/disadvantaged.htm.
Alternatively, go to:
http://www.inlandrevenue.gov.uk/so/pcode_search.htm

which allows postcodes to be entered to check if within a DDA.

You can also enquire about DDAs or *Enterprise Areas* by phoning the Stamp Taxes Helpline on 0845 603 0135. Poor or neglected areas are clearly more likely to be in a DDA than millionaires' row.

Tip

Solicitors usually add about £50 - £70 to their conveyancing fees charged to the Buyer for arranging payment of stamp duty. The Buyer can save this money by arranging this payment himself. Simply go to

http://www.inlandrevenue.gov.uk/so/sdlt_website.htm *and follow the on-screen instructions. Alternatively, telephone the Inland Revenue, 0845 302 1472, and obtain the forms for paying stamp duty by post. Remember to tell your solicitor that you will be filling in and making the SDLT payment direct to Inland Revenue and you therefore do not want to be charged for this service. The form is simple to fill in, and easy-to-follow guidance notes are given with the form. If you get stuck, you can telephone Inland Revenue for guidance (0845 6030135). The form should be filled in and submitted **after completion** of purchase because the date of completion must be entered on the form. Therefore, you will need to receive a completion statement from your solicitor before completing the form. Before deciding whether to do it yourself, have a look at a blank form and the guidance notes that come with it.*

You probably won't get the stamp duty exemption unless you ask for it, and more often than not home buyers do not ask. There have been many cases of people paying stamp duty unnecessarily in DDAs and never getting refunds. This happens because some solicitors may not be aware of the tax exemption, and because the tax authorities do not automatically check stamp duty payments against DDA records to give refunds.

Summary of *The Tax Exemption Strategy For Buyers*:

1. In the UK there are many DDAs (Designated Disadvantaged Areas). Any property bought in a DDA is exempt from stamp duty if the value is not over £150,000.

2. DDAs tend to be more common in poor or neglected areas, in both rural and urban communities. To check if a property

might be located in a DDA telephone 0845 603 0135, or go to
http://www.inlandrevenue.gov.uk/so/disadvantaged.htm

3. If taking advantage of a DDA as a Buyer, be sure to tell your
   solicitor so that you won't have to pay stamp duty.

The Threshold Strategy For Buyers

This strategy is about not paying a higher rate of stamp duty unless you legally have to. For properties priced close to the first threshold of £120,000 it may be possible to pay no stamp duty at all.

As mentioned, the rates of stamp duty are as follows:

Property Price	Stamp Duty
Not more than £120,000	0%
More than £120,000 but not more than £250,000	1%
More than £250,000 but not more than £500,000	3%
More than £500,000	4%

In this strategy we will be concerned with three tax thresholds:

- Paying nil duty instead of 1% duty.
- Paying 1% duty instead of 3% duty.
- Paying 3% duty instead of 4% duty.

For instance, a property priced at £250,000 incurs stamp duty at 1% (£2,500). But a property priced at £250,001 incurs stamp duty at 3% (£7,500.03). So just by moving down to a lower threshold by making a small change in the price, the potential savings can amount to thousands of pounds.

It therefore does not make sense to buy a property priced just over the threshold of £250,000. In fact you will rarely find properties priced in the £251,000 - £260,000 bracket precisely for this reason. A similar analogy applies to the £500,000 threshold.

In practice, Estate Agents and Sellers tend to avoid offering prices in the £250-£260k bracket, but you sometimes see prices at £259,000 or £260,000. The first £15,000 after the threshold tends to be 'forbidden territory'. In other words there are few properties priced between £250,000 and £265,000. This can be verified by looking in any property newspaper and in estate agents windows.

We can take advantage of this. Fig.3 shows how.

FIG. 3 - THE THRESHOLDS

OMV = Open Market Value
THRESHOLDS = £120,000 or £250,000 or £500,000, whichever most applies to your property deal.

Item	Seller's Perceived OMV (£)	Seller's asking price (£)	Potential price reduction (£)
1	Under the threshold	Under the threshold	May or may not be negotiable
2	Less than 2% over the threshold	The threshold price	Not very negotiable
3	Between 2% and 4% over the threshold	Between 2% and 4% over the threshold	Very negotiable
4	Between 4% and 10% over the threshold	Between 4% and 10% over the threshold	Not very negotiable
5	More than 10% over the threshold	More than 10% over the threshold	The threshold strategy becomes irrelevant

Item 1 in Fig. 3 shows that if the Seller/agent thinks the OMV (Open Market Value) is, for example, under £250,000, the stamp duty threshold of £250,000 is irrelevant and the price may or may not be negotiable.

Item 2 in Fig. 3 shows that if the Seller/agent thinks the OMV is, for example, £253,000 a price reduction is unlikely to be granted as the price has already been reduced to £250,000 to bring it below the stamp duty threshold.

Items 3 in Fig 3 show that if the Seller/agent thinks the OMV is, for example, £257,000, and the asking price is £257,000, there is a good chance of negotiating the price down to £250,000 because the Seller/agent knows this will save the Buyer significant stamp duty. In another example, if the Seller/agent thinks the OMV is, £125,000, and the asking price is £125,000, there is a good chance of negotiating the price down to £120,000 and avoiding stamp duty altogether.

Item 4 in Fig. 3 shows that if the Seller/agent thinks the OMV is, for example, £267,500 a price reduction to £250,000 is unlikely to be granted because it would be too big a reduction. The Seller/agent has decided to not take the stamp duty threshold into account in setting a selling price as it would be too much of a 'sacrifice'. However, there is still the possibility of negotiating a discount, but not enough to reach the lower threshold.

Item 5 in Fig 3 shows that if the Seller/agent thinks the OMV is, for example, £280,000, a price reduction to £250,000 is likely to be out of the question, and therefore the threshold strategy cannot be used.

The strategy then is to shortlist properties priced *over the threshold* but within about 4% of the threshold price. For example, any properties between £121,000 and £125,000 offer good chances of negotiating a price reduction down to £120,000. Similarly, for properties between £251,000 and £260,000. Or between £500,000 and £520,000.

Also remember that properties offered at just below the tax threshold, e.g. £249,500, may well have been reduced from a higher price in order to get a sale *without stamp duty being an objection*. Therefore, properties priced in this way may offer good bargains.

Here is an example of how the negotiation might go:

EXAMPLE

Buyer: '*You are selling the house for £259,000 is that correct?*'

Seller: '*Yes, the price is £259,000 and includes all the fixtures and fittings already discussed.*'

Buyer: '*Well, as you may know I would have to pay £7,770 in stamp duty on a price of £259,000 so I have a proposition. May I explain my proposed offer?*'

Seller: '*Please go ahead, I'm always open to offers.*'

Buyer: '*If I buy your house for £259,000 I will have to pay £7,770 stamp duty (and that's without taking into account solicitor fees, valuation fees, and the like). I therefore want to ask if you can accept £250,000?* [Explain the stamp duty implications]. *If you can agree to this, I will buy a list of chattels from your house for £5,000. This means you will get a total sum of £255,000 for your house.*'

Seller: '*Assuming we can agree a list of contents, how would you pay me the £5,000?*'

Buyer: '*My solicitor will confirm to your solicitor that I have agreed to buy a list of chattels from you, and the additional £5,000 would be paid upon completion. So you will get the £5,000 on the same day that the completion of sale goes through.*'

Seller: '*That sounds good. We may have a deal. Let's talk about the list of chattels.*'

Here are some tips for preparing the list of chattels:

- Take care that any amounts allocated to 'Chattels', such as carpets and curtains, are properly supportable. So in this example, the items listed need to reflect a realistic value of £5,000 in the eyes of the tax authorities. Of course, the Seller may only give the items a value of £500. The lower the perceived value for the Seller the better, as the £5,000 will then be more highly appreciated.

- Fixtures and fittings are not allowed as they are taxable. Therefore, only chattels (things that can be moved) are allowable.

- The List must be genuine, and the goods on the list must exist, even though the transaction might be viewed as a vehicle for paying money to the Seller (in this example £5,000). The Buyer should not try to 'get his money's worth'. Rather, he should try to help the Seller find the right balance between a worthless list and a supportable list.

- As many items as possible should be included on the list, however inconsequential and small the value. For example, include, if possible, all kitchen appliances and equipment. The longer the list the better.

- Do not enter money values for each item. Only enter the total value (e.g. £5,000).

- Do not enter terms such as 'fixtures and fittings' or 'floor coverings' or 'kitchen appliances' or 'Chattels'. Avoid generic names. Enter an individual name/description for each item.

Warning

The UK tax authorities do not like property transactions that include a large payment for 'chattels' (also known as 'movables') as a way of avoiding stamp duty. In particular they are likely to challenge and investigate a payment for chattels if the amount exceeds 10% of the price of the property. To play safe, any payment for chattels should not exceed 5% of the price of the property. Furthermore, the items sold as chattels must be worth the amount paid. Therefore, the more substantive the list of items the better.

In the above example the buyer would pay £257,500 for the house (£250,000 plus 1% stamp duty, plus £5,000). This compares against £266,770 without a reduction (£259,000 plus 3% stamp duty). So, as a result of negotiating a lower price, a saving of £9,270 has been made!

Note that the Seller ended up getting £255,000 instead of £259,000, a mere difference of £4,000 compared to the buyer's savings of £9,270.

Is it legal to offer to buy chattels in this way? Yes it is provided the chattels are genuine. This is what the tax authorities have to say on the matter (the following is a summarized extract from the Inland Revenue):

'For an item to be regarded as a fixture as opposed to a chattel (called 'movable' in Scotland), the item must be fixed to the property. Where a purchaser agrees to buy a property for a price that includes an amount properly attributed to chattels, that amount will not be charged to Stamp Duty.

In recent times an increasing number of cases have arisen in which the amount of money attributed to chattels is more than a small percentage of the total amount. This has been particularly noticeable where the chargeable amount is brought just below the £250,000 or £500,000 stamp duty thresholds.

Under the Stamp Duty regime a "just and reasonable apportionment" is required where a price is paid partly for a property and partly for chattels. It does not matter that the parties to a transaction may agree a particular apportionment, which is then documented in the contract. The apportionment will not be correct unless it was arrived at on a "just and reasonable" basis.

The Inland Revenue has the right to make enquiries into the property transaction and into cases where a deduction has been made for chattels, to confirm that those items properly fall within the definition of chattels. The Inland Revenue is unable to provide a comprehensive list of items that it accepts as chattels because each case must be considered on its own merits and because this is an area of the law that continues to evolve.

The following are, however, confirmed as being items that will normally be regarded as chattels:

- *Carpets (fitted or otherwise).*
- *Curtains and Blinds.*
- *Free-standing furniture.*
- *Kitchen white goods.*

- *Electric and Gas fires (provided that they can be removed by disconnection from the power supply without causing damage to the property).*
- *Light shades and fittings (unless recessed).*
- *Plants and shrubs growing in pots or containers (internally or externally).*

On the other hand, the following will <u>not</u> normally be regarded as chattels:

- *Fitted kitchen units, cupboards and sinks.*
- *Gas ovens and wall-mounted ovens.*
- *Fitted bathroom sanitary ware.*
- *Central heating systems.*
- *Intruder alarm systems.*
- *Plants, shrubs or trees growing in the soil.*

It is clear, then, that the tax authorities will allow a separate payment from Buyer to Seller for 'Chattels' provided that any stamp-duty-avoidance is incidental to the transaction rather than the sole purpose. It is also clear that such chattels may include fitted carpets, white kitchen goods, fitted curtains, removable gas and electric fires, and many items which traditionally have been thought of as 'fixtures and fittings'.

In fact the term 'fixtures and fittings' should never come into the transaction at any point, as matters can get confused. It is best to only think in terms of chattels (or 'movables' in Scotland).

There is a misconception that the value of 'fixtures and fittings' must be accounted for and added to the price of the property for stamp duty purposes. This is not so. The tax authorities regard fixtures and fittings as a taxable part of the property. If fixtures and fittings are charged for separately this cost must be added to the selling price, and stamp duty will be payable on the grand total. Therefore, the tax authorities do not care whether fixtures and fittings are included in the price or charged for separately since it makes no difference to the amount of tax paid.

In practice, fixtures and fittings will normally be included in the SELLING PRICE and therefore do not need to be 'evaluated'. However, the fixtures and fittings do need to be listed and agreed so that there can be no misunderstanding over what the Seller is or is not leaving behind. This is standard practice, and solicitors use a ready made check list when agreeing fixtures and fittings.

The point about *The Threshold Strategy For Buyers* is that fixtures and fittings cannot be used as a means of paying money to the Seller, *but chattels can.* This is what it boils down to:

- A Buyer gets taxed on non-chattels (i.e. fixtures) and they <u>cannot be</u> used to negotiate a below-threshold price.

- A Buyer does not get taxed on chattels and they <u>can be</u> used to negotiate a below-threshold price (but to be safe don't pay more than 5% of the SELLING PRICE for chattels).

- Make sure that as many items as possible are listed as chattels rather than as 'fixtures and fittings'. That way the chattels list will be more substantial and acceptable to the tax authorities.

A final point to remember is this: *Generally, be inclined to ask for a price reduction on any property priced over the threshold, but within about 4% of the threshold. They provide opportunities for good price reductions. Knowing this valuable tip can save you thousands of pounds.*

Summary of *The Threshold Strategy For Buyers*:

1. Use *The Threshold Strategy* to negotiate big price reductions. Alternatively, use this strategy in combination with other stamp-duty-avoidance strategies to make big savings.

2. Shortlist several properties that meet your criteria and fall within the chosen *price threshold*. Prepare the figures to be negotiated, and negotiate <u>direct with the Seller</u>. If an estate agent is involved, ask the agent to let you negotiate direct with the Seller (assure the agent that he will not be bypassed in any way and that his agency commission will

not be affected). If this is not possible, try to do it through a telephone conference with all three parties on the line. As a last resort negotiate with the Seller *through* the estate agent.

3. Prepare a CHATTELS LIST – a list of things that you can pay for separately (see above example). The longer the list the better. Make sure that no possible chattels get included on the 'fixtures and fittings' list prepared by the solicitor. Use the chattels list in your negotiations. Think of the chattels list as a vehicle for paying money to the Seller.

4. Consider your property budget (the price range you can pay) and establish which stamp duty threshold is most applicable. Then keep an eye on the property market for properties priced just over the threshold. Do this to seek out opportunities to negotiate good price reductions.

Stamp Duty Avoidance Strategy No. 3:

The Link Strategy For Buyers

This strategy will reduce the amount of stamp duty from 4% to 3%, from 3% to 1% (or even from 4% to 1%), giving a huge potential saving. It will only suit a property Buyer who may want to buy more than one property from the same Seller, either as a lot, or as a series of transactions over time. It will also suit anybody buying at auction.

The Link Strategy For Buyers helps you avoid falling into a *stamp duty tax trap,* a trap that most people have never heard of. Just about every week of the year people fall into this tax trap and end up paying much more stamp duty than they need to.

THE TAX TRAP

If buying two or more properties from the same person or company there is a likelihood that the transaction will be regarded as 'linked' for stamp duty tax purposes. This is so even if there is a time gap between each property transaction. For example, if buying two properties each priced at £150,000, the stamp duty rate would be 3% for each property rather than 1% (because, in this example, the total of £300,000 is above the stamp duty threshold of £250,000). In this example, the *extra* stamp duty you pay is £6,000. By using *The Link Strategy For Buyers,* you can potentially make savings of tens of thousands of pounds, depending on the prices of the properties.

As you can see, when the linked rule comes into play the extra stamp duty paid can be very substantial. If there is any possibility that you will be buying further properties from the same source (at any future date) or more than one property from the same person, it is important to be aware of *linked transactions* (the tax trap).

Section 108 of *The Finance Act 2003* has a section titled 'Linked Transactions' which reads as follows:

108   Linked transactions

(1) Transactions are "linked" for the purposes of this Part if they form part of a single scheme, arrangement or series of transactions between the same vendor and purchaser or, in either case, persons connected with them.

Section 839 of the Taxes Act 1988 (connected persons) has effect for the purposes of this subsection

(2) Where there are two or more linked transactions with the same effective date, the purchaser, or all of the purchasers if there is more than one, may make a single land transaction return as if all of those transactions that are notifiable were a single notifiable transaction.

(3) Where two or more purchasers make a single return in respect of linked transactions, section 103 (joint purchasers) applies as if-
(a) the transactions in question were a single transaction, and
(b) those purchasers were purchasers acting jointly.

What this means is that if you are buying more than one property from the same Seller, then according to *The Finance Act 2003*, the transaction is linked and you have to pay stamp duty *at a rate* based on the *total value* of all the properties being purchased.

However, there are circumstances when there is no linkage even though you may be buying more than one property from the same person or company. And when there is no linkage you do not get clobbered with extra stamp duty! What are these circumstances? Here are some examples:

Example 1.

A house builder is selling flats. He makes a special offer: *'Buy two flats and you get a discount of 15% on the second flat'.* Peter buys the two flats and *benefited* from the discount. This kind of transaction is linked because they are both part of the same business deal. The stamp duty rate is therefore based on the total value of both flats (resulting in a big jump in stamp duty!).

Alternative scenario.

A house builder is selling flats. He makes a special offer: 5% discount plus stamp duty paid. Peter buys one flat on these terms. Then a week later (or a month later, or a year later) Peter sees an advertisement from the builder offering further flats for sale, based on the same terms: 5% discount plus stamp duty paid. Peter responds to the advertisement in writing, making reference to the advertisement, and making no reference to any other property deals. In this alternative scenario there is no link because there was *no awareness* of further flats being available until Peter saw the advertisement. When it came to buying the second property, the Buyer *did not benefit* from his association with the first property deal or with the Seller because he got no special terms based on a second purchase. In this alternative scenario the two key phrases are *no awareness* and *no benefit*. When there is *no awareness* and *no benefit*, there is no link.

Example 2.

A house builder is selling flats. He sells a flat to Peter at £150,000. Peter is so pleased with the deal that he goes back to the Builder a month later and buys a second flat. This kind of transaction is linked because they are both part of the same business deal, or series of business deals. Peter's decision to buy a second flat is *linked* to his awareness of the first flat. The time gap of a month is immaterial – what counts here is the fact that the Buyer had knowledge that linked both transactions. When Peter bought the second flat he *benefited* from his knowledge of the first flat and from his association with the Seller. The stamp duty rate is therefore based on the total value of both flats. This means a portion of the stamp duty payable is 'backdated' to the first property.

Alternative scenario.

Let's suppose that the house builder sells a flat to Peter at £150,000. Peter is so pleased with the flat that he asks a friend to act as a scout and find him another flat in a similar price range. Peter has complete confidence in his friend and gives him full discretion to put down a reservation fee if he finds the right property. His friend does indeed find a great property and pays the reservation fee of £500. Peter is happy with this second deal but discovers a week later that the Seller is by coincidence the same person that sold him the first flat. In this alternative scenario there is no link because there was *no awareness* of the common ownership. Furthermore, Peter can provide documentary evidence showing that he instructed his friend to act for him. When it came to buying the second property, the Buyer *did not benefit* from his acquaintance with the owner of the first property. In this alternative scenario the two key phrases are *no awareness* and *no benefit*. When there is *no awareness* and *no benefit*, there is no link.

Example 3.

John is a developer and he sells a house to Peter. About a year later, John contacts Peter and tells him he has another good property to offer him; this time it's a flat. Peter buys the flat and rents it out. This kind of transaction is linked because they are both part of a series of business deals. The one-year time gap is immaterial. The stamp duty rate is therefore based on the total value of the house and the flat. This means a higher rate of stamp duty, and a portion of the stamp duty payable is 'backdated' to the first property.

Alternative scenario.

John is a developer and he sells a house to Peter. About a year later Peter decides he would like to buy a flat to rent out. He places an advertisement in the *property wanted* section of a suitable newspaper. John happens to see the advertisement and replies to it in writing, making reference to the advertisement. A deal is negotiated and Peter buys the flat without any reference to the house that he also purchased from John a year ago. In this alternative scenario there is no link because there was *no awareness* of the common ownership until John replied to the advertisement. Furthermore, Peter can provide documentary evidence showing that he advertised for a property and that John responded *in writing* to the advertisement. When it came to buying the second property, the Buyer *did not benefit* from his acquaintance with the owner of the first property. In this alternative scenario the two key phrases are *no awareness* and *no benefit*. When there is *no awareness* and *no benefit*, there is no link.

Example 4.

Peter buys a bungalow from John's building firm. A year later Peter sees an advertisement from John's firm offering a flat for sale. Peter responds to the advertisement without remembering that a year earlier he had dealt with the same firm for the purchase of his bungalow. Peter has not benefited from any discounts or special offers even though he is buying from John for the second time. In fact, Peter got exactly the same terms as if he were buying from John for the first time (absolutely no special terms whatsoever).

This kind of transaction is linked because they are both part of a series of business deals. The one-year time gap is immaterial. The stamp duty rate is therefore based on the total value of the bungalow and the flat. This means a portion of the stamp duty payable is 'backdated' to the first bungalow. Peter cannot argue that he did not benefit from, and was not aware of, the common ownership. The fact is that the two deals are linked by virtue of having the same Seller, and Peter cannot prove otherwise. Without documentary proof you have no case because a 'linked transaction' is assumed unless you can prove otherwise.

Alternative scenario.

Peter buys a bungalow from John's building firm. A year later Peter goes to a property auction and buys a flat from John. Later Peter discovers that the flat bought at auction was owned by the same John that sold him a bungalow a year ago. Clearly, Peter was not aware that John was the owner at the time of bidding for the property, and clearly Peter never suggested to John that he should sell the flat at auction. In this alternative scenario there is no link because there was *no awareness* of the common ownership. When it came to buying the second property at auction, the Buyer *did not benefit* from his association with the first property or with the Seller. In this alternative scenario the two key phrases are *no awareness* and *no benefit*. When there is *no awareness* and *no benefit*, there is no link.

Example 5.

Peter is interested in buying two run-down flats in a city centre building. He checks them out through the estate agent and is informed *in writing* that they are both owned by *City Banking Corporation*, as a result of a repossession. Peter goes to the property auction and successfully bids for the first flat. He decides he will try his luck and go for the second flat, and again he wins the bid. This kind of transaction is linked because they are both part of a succession of business deals. In any investigation by the tax authorities they will quickly discover that the estate agent informed Peter about the common ownership of the two flats. The stamp duty rate is therefore based on the total value of both flats (resulting in a big jump in stamp duty!).

Alternative scenario.

Peter is interested in buying two run-down flats in a city centre building. He checks them out through the estate agent but is not told who the owner is or that they both belong to the same owner. There is nothing in the paperwork or the Auction House brochure to indicate that both flats have a common owner. Peter buys both properties at auction.

Later he discovers that both properties were owned by the *City Banking Corporation*. In this alternative scenario there is no link because there was *no awareness* of the common ownership. When it came to buying the second property at auction, the Buyer *did not benefit* from knowing he had just bought the first flat. In this alternative scenario the two key phrases are *no awareness* and *no benefit*. When there is *no awareness* and *no benefit*, there is no link.

Example 6.

Peter wants to buy two flats from John. For buying two flats Peter gets a special 5% discount on each flat. This is a linked transaction so stamp duty is paid at 3% instead of 1%. However, by getting 5% discount Peter is better off even though he has to pay the additional stamp duty. Peter therefore goes ahead with the deal on the basis of it being a linked transaction.

Alternative scenario.

Peter wants to buy two flats from a John. However, he decides that he will buy just one flat and he negotiates a 10% discount. A week later Peter sees an advertisement from John and as a result of *seeing the advertisement* Peter decides to buy another flat. He tells his solicitor <u>in writing</u> that as a result of seeing the advertisement he wants to buy a property from John (throughout the proceedings Peter and John make no reference to any other property deals). So Peter goes ahead and buys the second flat *without any discount.* Each transaction has been 'negotiated' separately with nothing to link them. Peter did *not use his awareness* of the first transaction to derive a benefit from the second transaction: as no discount was given *no benefit* was obtained. Furthermore, at the time of buying the first property, Peter *did not contemplate* buying a second property. As this is not a linked transaction, stamp duty is only paid at the rate of 1% (rather than 3%) for each property. The net result is that Peter bought two properties, paid stamp duty at 1%, and obtained a 10% discount on one of them.

Example 7.

This example shows how a Buyer can use *The Link Strategy For Buyers* to buy two or more properties from the same Seller, without falling into the *linked transaction* trap (and with financial gain for both parties).

Scenario A (not using the strategy):

Peter has been watching a property development and wants to buy two (or more) flats in a new-build block. The price of each flat is £160,000. Peter negotiates with the Seller and agrees to buy two flats at £150,000 each. As this is a linked transaction the Buyer pays £300,000, plus stamp duty at 3% = £9,000. The Seller receives £300,000.

The total costs for Buyer and Seller are as follows:

Table A

Total costs incurred by Buyer	Total money received by Seller
Two flats at £150,000 each = £300,000 Plus stamp duty @ 3% = £9,000 TOTAL: £309,000	Two flats at £150,000 each = £300,000 (Stamp duty of £9,000 paid by Buyer) TOTAL: £300,000

Alternative Scenario B:

Peter has been watching a property development and wants to buy two (or more) flats in a new-build block. The asking price of each flat is £160,000. Peter negotiates with the Seller and this is what happens:

- Peter buys one flat only at the full asking price of £160,000.

- The Seller agrees to pay the cost of stamp duty amounting to £1,600.

- The Seller also agrees to give the Buyer a cash incentive amounting to £7,000 (this is less than 5% of the price).

- The deal goes through as a single unconditional transaction (it is not part of any kind of multiple deal and no reference is made to the possibility that further business will transpire).

- Later (say two weeks later), the Buyer is surprised to see an advertisement stating that another flat has become available from the Seller. Alternatively, the Buyer is surprised to receive a letter from a friend telling him about an opportunity to buy a flat. As a result of this (documented) turn of events, Peter goes ahead and buys a second property on the same terms as before. This means two separate transactions have taken place with no linkage in terms of benefits and awareness between the two transactions.

- The total cost for Buyer and Seller would therefore be as shown in Table B:

Table B

Total costs incurred by Buyer	Total money received by Seller
Two flats at £160,000 each = £320,000	Two flats at £160,000 each = £320,000
(Stamp duty of £3,200 is paid by Seller)	Less stamp duty @ 1% = £3,200
Less £14,000 cash incentives = £14,000	Less £14,000 cash incentive = £14,000
TOTAL: £306,000	TOTAL: £302,800

- This means the Seller would get £2,800 more than otherwise, plus he would be able to offer a similar package to other customers if he wished to, as a way of generating more business.

- The buyer would benefit by paying a total of £306,000 instead of £309,000, plus having the flexibility to give the Seller repeat business without getting clobbered with excessive stamp duty.

Note: The cash incentive would be paid by the Seller to the Buyer from the proceeds of sale. This would be done on completion of sale by the Seller's solicitor. If buying with a mortgage, the Buyer would declare the cash incentive on the mortgage application form. Lenders do not mind this, provided the valuation carried out by the Lender is in agreement with the selling price.

In this example, Peter ensures that each property transaction is carried out separately with absolutely no linkage. This means there is no mention of discounts or benefits for buying two or more properties and everything possible is done to keep separate each property sale (separate paperwork, separate conveyancing, separate purchase date for each property) so that there is no link between each property sale.

In comparing above tables A and B you can see that both parties have benefited. The Seller has been able to find a buyer, sell two (or more) properties, and make a gain of £2,800 by agreeing to do business in a way that helps the Buyer avoid the *linked transaction* trap. (Note: The Buyer could also give the Seller a printed copy of this book and refer to the chapter titled *The Link Strategy For Sellers.*)

Note that in Scenario B (using the strategy) the Buyer comes out better even though paying £160,000 instead of £150,000 per flat!

What's happening here is that the savings in stamp duty (£3,200 instead of £9,000) are, in effect, being shared by the Buyer and the Seller, so both parties come out winning. The amount 'shared' by each party can be changed by simply changing the selling price or the cash incentive amount.

When buying several properties from a single source, the savings in stamp duty are very significant indeed. In this example, if buying just four flats from the same Seller at £160,000 each, the amount of potential stamp duty *savings* is £19,200! Note: In this example, Peter, the Buyer, is not cheating – he is doing this with a clear conscience because the correct stamp duty is being paid on each and every property transaction, and no multiple transaction has taken place.

Example 8.

Peter buys a flat in a high rise building at £190,000, plus a parking bay in the basement at £18,000. This is regarded as a linked transaction because both properties are being purchased from the same Seller as part of a single arrangement or series of transactions. It does not matter whether the parking bay is a specific allocated bay or whether you are just buying the right to use any space in the car park. The stamp duty payable is therefore 1% of £208,000.

Alternative Scenario.

Peter buys a flat in a high rise building at £190,000 and pays stamp duty at 1%. A month (or a year) later the same Seller contacts Peter and offers him a parking bay that has become available. This is not a linked transaction, because at the time of buying the flat Peter was not contemplating buying a parking bay and he was not aware that a parking bay was available. Furthermore, there is no documentary evidence to prove otherwise. Peter decides to accept the Seller's offer, and he buys the parking bay for £18,000. As this is not a linked transaction, Peter pays no stamp duty on the £18,000 because the amount is below the tax threshold of £120,000.

Note that if you are buying property at auction and it is not the first time you have done so, you have to be extremely careful about how you proceed if there is any possibility that you are dealing with the same Seller. Should it be the same Seller, you want to be able to prove (with documentary evidence) that you did *not benefit from* and had *no awareness of* the common ownership. Then, should the tax authorities investigate, you can prove your case.

Another point is that a husband and wife are regarded as linked. You cannot buy one property from the husband and another from his wife as a way of avoiding a linked transaction. The linkage between spouses also extends to immediate family. When it comes to other relatives or work colleagues, the law is vague in terms of what constitutes a 'connected person' so be wary.

To police matters relating to linked transactions, the Inland Revenue has set up a special department that is informally known as 'COP 10' (coppers come to mind!). COP 10 refers to the Inland Revenue *Code Of Practice* number 10 (a kind of charter). You can see the text of this charter on the Internet by going to **http://www.inlandrevenue.gov.uk/pdfs/cop10.htm**.

Should the tax authorities suspect possible linkage, the matter would typically be referred to COP 10 for investigation. The COP 10 code of practice explains how they investigate linked transactions and what documents and information would be required in the event of a query.

These documents are:

- your name and tax reference number;
- full particulars of the transaction or event in question;
- copies of all relevant documents with the relevant parts or passages identified;
- your opinion of the tax consequences of the particular transaction;

- your explanation of the particular point(s) of difficulty that led to your request;
- details of what sections of the Taxes Acts you consider to be relevant;
- particulars of any case law, Inland Revenue extra-statutory concessions or Statements of Practice you consider to be relevant;
- your reasons for your opinion of the tax consequences of the transaction.

Typically, COP 10 can rule on whether a particular property transaction is to be regarded as linked or not linked for stamp duty purposes. Naturally, if you were to discuss a particular scenario *before* the event, it must be entirely hypothetical. You can hardly claim at a later date that you had no **awareness** if you previously discussed it with COP 10, so tread with caution! COP 10 can be contacted as follows (this address acts for the whole of the UK):

COP 10
Manchester Stamp Office
Upper Fifth Floor
Royal Exchange
Exchange Street
Manchester, M2 7EV

Tel: 0161 834 8109

It is important to know about COP 10 in case you ever have to deal with them. Clearly, if you are dealing with COP 10 you have to remember that you are, in effect, dealing with the Inland Revenue.

If the Inland Revenue became suspicious about a stamp duty payment it could result in enquiries being made by COP 10. This is what the tax authorities have to say about linked transactions vis-à-vis stamp duty:

'Section 108 of the Finance Act 2003 states that transactions are regarded as linked if they form part of a single scheme, arrangement or series of transactions between the same vendor(s) and purchaser(s) or parties connected with them. It is a matter of fact whether transactions are linked or not and the parties involved will be the best placed to make that judgment. Transactions do not have to be 'interdependent' in any legal sense in order to be linked. The fact that the transactions were contemplated at the same time is strong evidence that they are linked.

The way in which the transactions are documented is of much less importance that what precedes the documents. If transactions are negotiated together then this is strong evidence that they are linked. Even if they are negotiated one after the other they could well be linked if, e.g. the fact of the first one has affected the price for the second.

The classic 'non-linked' transaction is the purchase of separate lots at auction. Another example is the renewal of a lease following new negotiations between landlord and tenant. I should say in addition that we do not interpret a 'series of transactions' as just meaning that the transactions follow one after the other (such as the grant of a lease followed by its renewal five years later after new negotiations). They must be connected in some way.

If you are uncertain about the Inland Revenue's interpretation of the law (including its application to a proposed transaction) we [COP 10] will advise you if your query is in the following categories

- the interpretation of legislation passed in the last four Finance Acts ;

- the application of double taxation agreements;

- whether someone is employed or self employed;

- Statements of Practice and extra-statutory concessions;

- other areas concerning matters of major public interest in an industry or in the financial sector.

However, we will not help with tax planning, or advise on transactions designed to avoid or reduce the tax charge which might otherwise be expected to arise. And your query must arise from genuine uncertainty about the meaning of the law.'

This is what it boils down to: whenever you may be buying more than one property from the same Seller (with or without time gaps) make sure that you can pass the *link test:*.

FIG. 4 - THE LINK TEST

No awareness: At the time of purchase, you must not be contemplating buying more than one property (from the same Seller). Equally, you must not be aware of any other property purchase made in the past (from the same Seller). This must be backed up with crystal clear *documentary* evidence that is irrefutable.

No benefit: No benefit must be derived from a property purchase as a result of any other property purchase from the same Seller. This must be backed up with crystal clear documentary evidence that is irrefutable.

If there is awareness but no benefit, it will be regarded as a linked transaction unless you can clearly prove with documentary evidence that there was no benefit. Even then, the transaction may be regarded as linked by virtue of awareness alone.

If there was benefit but no awareness, it will be regarded as a linked transaction unless you can clearly prove with documentary evidence that there was no awareness. Even then, the transaction may be regarded as linked by virtue of benefit alone.

If there was no benefit and no awareness it will not be regarded as a linked transaction, but it is still very important to have irrefutable documentary evidence to back this up in case it is queried by the tax authorities.

34

Note that stamp duty is a self-assessment tax. That is, you the Buyer must decide the correct amount of stamp duty to pay, and you do this when filling in the stamp duty payment form. Council tax, for example, is not a self-assessment tax because the tax authorities check your home and then tell you exactly how much tax to pay.

In regard to linked transactions, the following questions come to mind:

1. *If I buy a property (either off-plan or ready built) does that mean I can never again buy another property from the same firm without being penalized with extra stamp duty? The answer is YES unless you can pass the link test* (see Fig. 4).

2. *Can I ever buy more than one property from the same Seller without being penalized with extra stamp duty? The answer is NO unless you can pass the link test* (see Fig. 4).

Section 108 'Linked Transactions' of The Finance Act 2003 is a pointless and pernicious bit of legislation that fully deserves to be abolished. It is pointless because it serves no purpose except to collect more tax from a product that is already taxed. It does not close any so called 'tax loophole' since property transactions that are not linked still get taxed with stamp duty in the usual way. It is pernicious because it serves to castigate bona fide property owners and business people who merely wish to buy more than one property from the same Seller. Furthermore, it goes against a fundamental principle of free enterprise: it discourages repeat business and customer loyalty by imposing tax penalties against this.

Finally, remember that in spite of following the advice in this chapter, it is always necessary for the Inland Revenue to believe you. If they don't you could potentially have an expensive fight on your hands. If you are in any doubt about how to proceed you should consult a solicitor.

Summary of *The Link Strategy For Buyers:*

1. Use this strategy to avoid paying additional stamp duty when buying more than one property from the same Seller (with or without time gaps).

2. Remember that a husband and wife are regarded as 'connected' and if buying property from both, it will be regarded as a linked transaction.

3. Study the examples given in this chapter to understand how not to fall into a linked transaction trap.

4. If you are planning a property deal that could be regarded as a linked transaction and you want to get clarification from the tax authorities before proceeding, be very careful! By discussing the deal with the tax authorities you may no longer be able to pass the *link test* for **awareness** for that particular deal.

5. If there is any possibility that you will be buying more than one property from the same Seller (now or in the future), make sure that you will be able to pass the *link test* (see Fig. 4) by studying this chapter and planning your strategy carefully.

The Mortgage Cashback Strategy For Buyers

When considering a mortgage you will be presented with many options, such as: fixed or variable interest, the rate of interest, with or without redemption penalties, interest only or capital repayment, and so on.

There is a bewildering range of mortgages from many different financial institutions, adding up to many possibilities for borrowing money. Before you start to look for a mortgage, your requirements need to be carefully worked out. Below is a simple check list to go through, to establish the kind of mortgage you might need (see Fig. 5 on the next page).

FIG. 5 - MORTGAGE CHECK LIST

'Comments' column shows issues to be considered to narrow down the kind of mortgage required

Item	Mortgage feature	Comments
1	Buy-to-let mortgage	Rental income needs to cover mortgage repayments
2	Own home mortgage	Will you be living there?
3	Interest only	Best for buy-to-let
4	Capital repayment	Best for own home mortgage
5	Fixed interest rate	Do you think interest rates will go up or down in the years to come?
6	Variable interest rate (also known as 'Standard Variable Rate')	Best if planning to sell soon. This is the best kind of mortgage to apply for if you want a mortgage cashback.
7	Deposit amount	e.g. 15% deposit paid by Buyer
8	No deposit	i.e. 100% mortgage
9	With redemption penalties?	Will the lender penalize you if the mortgage is repaid or remortgaged? Typically, redemption penalties apply for the first 1 to 3 years of mortgage. So if not planning to sell in short term, redemption penalties may not matter.
10	Self certification	Can you prove you are earning a salary? If not, or if self-employed, apply for a self certification mortgage.
11	Cashback	You get a cashback (i.e. a sum of money) given to you by the lender in addition to the loan for the property. Cashbacks typically range from £500 to £5,000 or more.

Fig. 5 is not a complete list of all the mortgage options available in the UK. But it is a useful check list: consider each item as it best applies to you and begin to narrow down the kind of mortgage you may need. You must get a rough idea about the kind of mortgage you can apply for *before* you start hunting for a property to buy. Once you have found a property you will then be able to negotiate a better price knowing what kind of mortgage you are likely to get.

The Mortgage Cashback Strategy For Buyers involves getting a mortgage that gives a cashback (i.e. a lump sum of money) that can be used towards your property purchase costs or anything else. Note that the cashback comes from the Lender, not from the Seller (later in this book we talk about a 'Cashback').

For a good general introduction to the mortgage scene in the UK go to the Motley Fool website at:

http://www.fool.co.uk/mortgages/articles/mortgagebasics.htm.

This is what they have to say about cashbacks:

> *'Some of the instant inducements include the offer of a lump sum in cash once the forms are signed. The 'cashback', as it's called, can obviously be useful if you haven't got any spare money to pay for furniture or legal fees or moving costs. However, as always, watch out for the small print. Some providers reserve the right to claim part of this money back if you switch mortgages within a certain timescale.'*

Cashback deals are usually available only on loans with standard variable rates. As many Lenders in the UK offer mortgage cashbacks you should take full advantage provided the redemption penalties are acceptable. To find out the kind of cashback you can get proceed as follows:

1. Go to a mortgage broker who will not charge for his services. To find a 'free' broker look in Yellow Pages under 'Mortgages'. Most mortgage brokers are free because they get paid commission by the Lender when they arrange a mortgage. Since they get commission from just about all Lenders, they can afford to be impartial in their advice to you.

2. See a broker *before* you have found a property to buy, so that you can get the mortgage set up in advance. Endeavour to fill

in any forms as far as possible, to determine the kind of mortgage you might need (this will save time later when getting the mortgage).

3. Tell the broker that you want a mortgage to buy a property (explain why you want to buy a property, is it buy-to-let, will you be re-selling, how much deposit will you be paying, and so on). Ask the broker to show you some good examples of the kind of mortgage that would suit you.

4. Tell the broker you are interested in cashback mortgages and see what can be offered. You may find that a good cashback mortgage goes hand-in-hand with a not-so-good interest rate, or a not-so-good redemption penalty (it's swings and roundabouts). But interest rates may not matter that much if you are planning to re-sell soon. Equally, redemption penalties may not matter if you are planning to keep the property for several years without remortgaging. The point is this: go for as big a cashback as you can get if the other factors in the mortgage deal are acceptable.

Tip

You can save thousands of pounds over the term of a mortgage by not buying 'buildings insurance' from a high-street lender. Instead, get insurance cover from smaller companies like Berkeley Alexander (01273 812922) or Payment Shield (0870 7594000). You are not obliged to get insurance from the same lender that is giving you a mortgage, or even from a company recommended by your Lender.

Some mortgage brokers will be able to find deals that offer up to 7.5% mortgage cashback – this can amount to fifteen or twenty thousand pounds! Beware the small print, as there may be stiff 'penalties' in terms of redemption penalties, interest rates, deposit requirements, and so on. A good way to gauge a cashback mortgage is to get the details of a good mortgage deal that meets your requirements *without* any cashback. Then use this as a template for comparing mortgage deals that offer cashbacks.

A redemption penalty is the main 'sting in the tail' applied to mortgage cashback offers. The term 'redemption penalty' refers to the cost you will have to pay the Lender if you decide to pay off your mortgage or switch to another mortgage company.

Redemption penalties are usually for a fixed term, e.g. three years, and then disappear.

Do not be put off by redemption penalties. They can be perfectly acceptable if, for instance, you are buying a home and you have no plans to remortgage or move home again in the near future. Provided you understand and accept the terms of the redemption penalty (and other aspects of the mortgage), it makes sense to go for the biggest mortgage cashback you can get.

Some Lenders offer cashbacks in the form of 'free gifts' – a growing trend in the UK. For example, at the time of this publication, West Bromwich Building Society offers a free Rover car instead of a cashback (with a redemption penalty that lasts five years).

Also, consider the alternative of getting a *remortgage cashback*. In this scenario, you would remortgage your home or some other property that you already own, get a cashback, and use the remortgage money to purchase a property for cash.

Although we are talking about getting cashbacks from *Lenders*, you can sometimes get small cashbacks from *mortgage brokers*. Once you've decided on a mortgage product it is worth considering purchasing it through a mortgage broker. As UK mortgage brokers receive commission for selling financial products, they will often split this money with you if asked. You can often get a cashback in the region of £100 - £300.

But remember that mortgage Brokers may not actually be able to offer the product you are looking for, so carefully consider alternatives offered. Don't be put off if the brokers can't provide what you have decided upon: carry on phoning around, or even get in touch with the mortgage company directly and ask them which brokers supply their mortgages.

Tip

If researching on the Internet, do not be tempted to fill in mortgage application forms online. Why? Because, every time you fill in a mortgage application form online (or even request a quotation online) the Lender or broker will automatically do a credit check on you. And every time a credit check is done it counts as a black mark on your credit rating (the less credit checks that go into your records the better).

To get an idea of what is available in the way of cashback mortgages check it out on the Internet. Here is a website that gives details of cashback mortgages: **http://www.marketplace.co.uk**

Other ways to get mortgage cashback information:

1. Check the local property newspapers for mortgage company and broker advertisements.

2. Check the national newspapers (every national newspaper has a particular day of the week when they focus on property and mortgage advertisements – usually a Friday or Saturday).

3. Buy the 'What Mortgage' magazine at just £3.20 from any good magazine retailer. This magazine is full of advice and mortgage offers that include cashbacks.

Most of the big mortgage companies offer basic mortgage cashbacks. A typical offer will be for a £500 cashback, to be repaid over three years. Other cashbacks have no repayment requirements, and amount to 'gifts'.

Summary of *The Mortgage Cashback Strategy For Buyers:*

1. Go for a cashback if the mortgage deal as a whole is acceptable, and use the cashback money to pay for **stamp duty** and other conveyancing costs.

2. Go for the largest cashback offer available, all things being equal.

3. Use a free mortgage broker to make a shortlist of two or three possible mortgage cashbacks suitable to your requirements. To find a broker see Yellow Pages under 'Mortgages'. Also, check the 'What Mortgage' magazine.

4. Do as much form filling as possible with the mortgage broker so that when the mortgage application is made for a particular property, time is saved. When you visit the broker *for the first time* take your passport and a utility bill (this will save time at a later stage).

5. Keep an eye on the mortgage market by using the internet, property newspapers, and magazines such as 'What Mortgage'.

The Price Strategy For Buyers

This is a great strategy for saving stamp duty costs and it applies to most situations involved in buying residential property. At this point you may want to review the chapter titled 'Financial Elements' to reiterate the terms used in this strategy.

Normally, when a PRICE is agreed between Buyer and Seller, this is the figure that goes on your mortgage application form. Provided that the valuation carried out by the Lender is not *less* than the PRICE, the Buyer will get a mortgage based upon this figure.

To explain further we will look at the following example:

Example

- Seller's asking price: £210,000.

- The rock bottom amount that the Seller is willing to accept: £200,000.

- Buyer only wants to pay £190,000, so there is a price gap of £10,000.

- Buyer can get a 95% Loan To Value mortgage.

- Deposit is therefore 5%.

In this example there is an impasse over the price. This is a common occurrence as Sellers often get offers below their asking price. If the Buyer and Seller cannot find common ground, the deal is lost and no sale goes ahead. But using *The Price Strategy For Buyers* this needn't be the case. We will compare two scenarios based on this example:

Scenario one, based on the *traditional approach*

- Asking price: £210,000

- Discounted amount (price after negotiation): £200,000.

- Mortgage amount is £190,000 (95% of £200,000).

- Mortgage Deposit (payment from Buyer to Buyer's Lender): £10,000 (5% of £200,000).

- Buyer has to pay stamp duty, legal fees, mortgage valuation, and all other costs out of his own resources as these cannot be included in the mortgage or property bank loan.

- Property would be registered at the land registry with a value of £200,000.

- Deal goes ahead if Buyer agrees a selling price of £200,000 and has enough savings to pay for the mortgage deposit, stamp duty, and all other conveyancing costs. In this scenario the deal is lost as the Buyer wants a price of £190,000.

Scenario two based on *The Price Strategy For Buyers*

- Asking price: £210,000

- Discounted amount (price agreed after negotiation): £200,000.

- Cash Incentive agreed (payment from Seller to Buyer): £10,000 (difference between £210,000 and £200,000, so Seller ends up getting £200,000 for house).

- Mortgage amount is £199,500 (95% of £210,000).

- Mortgage Deposit (payment from Buyer to Buyer's Lender): £10,500 (5% of £210,000).

- Buyer can pay for stamp duty, legal fees, mortgage valuation, and all other costs from the £10,000 cash incentive, and still have money left over.

- Property would be registered at the land registry with a value of £210,000.

- Deal goes ahead, based on a selling price of £210,000 because the Buyer has a cash incentive of £10,000 which greatly helps pay for the mortgage deposit, stamp duty, and all other conveyancing costs.

We will now look at scenario two in more detail and explain the strategy further. What follows is a step-by-step procedure, including suggested dialogue.

STEP 1: Negotiate a price.

STEP 2: Make an offer.

STEP 3: Confirm it in writing.

STEP 1: Negotiate a price.

- The Buyer will naturally negotiate the best price he can, and here we assume the price has been negotiated down to £200,000 in the 'conventional' manner. Hence, a £10,000 price reduction has been achieved (most Sellers will agree to reduce the price to some degree if they think they have found a buyer – it's just a matter of finding out the lowest price that the Seller is willing to come down to).

- Whether or not the Seller is willing to reduce the price, *The Price Strategy For Buyers* can be used to good effect. In any event, STEP 1 involves getting the best price you can *before* starting to use *The Price Strategy For Buyers.*

STEP 2: Make an offer.

You go on to this step only after one of the following has occurred:

- You have negotiated the best price you can get and a price reduction has been agreed in principle.

- You have negotiated the best price you can get and no price reduction was possible.

In this example we will assume that a price reduction from £210,000 to £200,000 is on offer from the Seller. Later we will cover a situation where no price reduction is available. You now start to apply the strategy.

You start by confirming the price reduction that has been agreed. You then go on to ask the Seller to agree the asking price of £210,000! This apparent *volte-face* may come as a surprise to the Seller, but the Buyer goes on to explain that the price to be paid will still only be £200,000. The dialogue would go along the lines that follow.

Note: Speak slowly when negotiating, don't rush things through. Also, pause after each 'chunk' of dialogue to make sure the Seller has heard you correctly, and make certain there are no misunderstandings. If you get any questions and you don't want to stop at that point, say *'I will go on to explain that in just a moment'.*

Dialogue:

- *'Now that we've agreed a price of £200,000, this is the amount I will be paying you. I like your house very much, and it shouldn't be devalued. I want to enter the full market value (in other words, the full asking price) on the Land Registry. Therefore I want to ask you to agree a selling price of £210,000. I also want to ask you to give me a Cash Incentive of £10,000. So you get paid £210,000, and you give me back £10,000. This means you will still be getting the agreed £200,000, but the house value will go through on the Land Registry as £210,000.'*

- *'The house price of £210,000 is the price that would go on all the paperwork including my mortgage application. The Cash Incentive of £10,000 will help me pay for legal fees, stamp duty and other costs, and in carrying out certain renovation work before I move in.'*

- *'This method of buying your house won't affect you in any way. On completion, my solicitor will give your solicitor the agreed selling price of £210,000. Your solicitor will then give my solicitor the agreed £10,000 Cash Incentive. Of course, you will need to tell your solicitor about this and I'll give you a letter for your solicitor which explains all this.'*

- *'All that we have discussed is completely legal and above board, and is common practice throughout the building industry. The £10,000 price difference is a cash incentive, and any experienced conveyancer will be familiar with this way of* doing business. *This £10,000 is a cash incentive from you to me but the money does not come from you – it comes from the money I am borrowing to buy your house.'*

- *'The cash incentive is, in effect, a payment from my Lender to me, but it goes through your solicitor. The following diagram shows how this works'.*

(See the diagram in Fig. 6 - give the Seller a copy, and go through it together).

FIG. 6 - MONEY-FLOW DIAGRAM

Step 1
LENDER
(money loaned to Buyer, based on selling price)

Step 2
BUYER'S SOLICITOR
(Money given to Buyer's solicitor for buying property)

Step 3
SELLER'S SOLICITOR
(Money paid to Seller's solicitor on completion, without deducting the cash incentive)

Step 4
BUYER'S SOLICITOR
(Seller's solicitor 'pays' cash incentive money to Buyer's solicitor for giving to Buyer)

Step 5
BUYER
Buyer receives cash incentive money as part of the final reconciliation of the completion statement prepared by Buyer's solicitor

---

To finish this point, explain that the cash incentive amounts to surplus money that is left over (the difference between the amount borrowed and the amount actually paid for the property). You now continue the dialogue to finish the negotiations.

- *'Have a look at these advertisements. What I am proposing is no different to the way large building companies operate. You and I are doing the same thing but on a smaller scale. In these advertisements, the building companies are selling directly to buyers, just as you are selling directly to me.'*

  (Show advertisements depicting cash incentive offers from builders like Barratt. Answer any remaining questions).

- *'If you can help me out by doing this I will be very pleased to buy your (fridge/curtains/sofa/flower pots/whatever) for £300. I will pay you cash for these items in a separate transaction. So you will end up getting the £200,000 payment for the house, and in addition you get a separate cash payment direct from me for £300.'*

  Make sure that you have established beforehand in your own mind which item (or items) you will be buying for £300. It needs to be an item of little value, or an item that would have been included in the price of the house anyway. That way, the £300 will be genuinely appreciated.

- *'If you will agree to this method of selling your property this is how you will benefit:*

  1. *'You get to sell your property at the agreed price.*

  2. *'You can stop looking for a buyer as you will now be able to sell your property. It means you can move on with other things in your life, knowing that you have sold this house.*

  3. *'Your property will not be devalued in the local market place as it will be registered at the higher value of £210,000. This can benefit you or your relatives who may own other properties in the area.*

  4. *'You get an additional £300 as a separate cash payment direct from me.'*

(Give the Seller a separate sheet showing these four benefits.)

- *'So can I take it that you agree in principle with this strategy? If so, I will give you a letter confirming my agreement to buy your house. I will also give you a letter that you can send to your solicitor which explains the strategy we have been talking about.'*

Stop to make sure the Seller has heard you correctly, and make certain there are no misunderstandings. At this point you must wait to get an answer to know whether or not the Seller is going to co-operate. Do not proceed to STEP 3, if it is clear that the Seller will not co-operate.

Summary of the Seller benefits:

1. Seller has found a Buyer and can sell the house.

2. Seller gets to sell the house at the desired price.

3. Seller's house is not devalued in the local market place (this can benefit the Seller if he/she owns other local properties, or has nearby relatives who own properties).

4. Seller gets an additional payment (£300 in this example) for co-operating with the strategy.

Summary of the Buyer benefits:

1. Buyer gets to buy the property at a bargain price because, as a result of getting the cash incentive, he paid much less than the registered price.

2. Buyer gets a property with equity, i.e. the potential profit that can be made when re-selling the property.

3. Buyer gets cash (in this example £10,000) that can be used to pay for stamp duty, legal fees, conveyancing costs, or just be put into a savings account!

The key to *The Price Strategy For Buyers* is the price difference between the 'official' price on which the mortgage is based and the actual amount paid to the Seller.   This difference is the *cash incentive*.   In the building industry it is common for house builders to offer cash incentives, and the amount of the cash incentive will have been factored into the selling price.   Hence, there is no legal difference between a cash incentive offered by a house builder and a cash incentive offered by a private individual as described in this strategy.

Provided the cash incentive is not more than 10% of the PRICE it will usually not be a cause for concern to anybody. If it is not over 5% (as in this example) it should be perfectly acceptable to all parties. However, cash incentives of 15% are not uncommon in the building industry.

Note: The Buyer may declare the *cash incentive* on his mortgage application form (there is nothing to hide). The Lender will not mind that the Buyer is getting a cash incentive provided the selling price is in line with the valuation report. Remember three things: (i) The *Cash Incentive* is not an additional loan from the Lender, (ii) the Lender is not involved with the cash incentive in any direct or legal sense, and (iii) Lenders themselves give cash incentives to Buyers (just look at any mortgage magazine).

A cash incentive received by a Buyer is not usually regarded as income and is should therefore be tax free. This is so because the amount is relatively small and is not part of an estate being inherited. The cashback is akin to a gift – if you receive a gift of money it is tax free, like winning the lottery! The only exception to this is a professional property trader. If you are in the business of buying and selling property for a living, then the *Cash Incentive* is regarded as income or profit and is therefore taxable, just like any other earned income. If a *Cash Incentive* is received by a Company, but not a property trading company, it may be taxable depending on the financial situation of the Company, and advice from a tax accountant may be appropriate.

Regarding Capital Gains Tax, this will not apply if buying or selling your own home (the place where you live). If the property is bought or sold by a property trader or investor, e.g. for re-selling or for buy-to-let, the following applies:

Buyer. If a property is bought at a higher price by virtue of getting a cash incentive, the Buyer who is a property investor will pay *less* capital gains tax if and when selling because the price *difference* will be that much less. Note that the capital gains amount is normally based on the difference between the buying price and the selling price as entered at the Land Registry. Hence, the *Cash Incentive* will ultimately have the effect of reducing the capital gains tax bill. But remember that capital gains tax is not applicable if buying or selling your own home.

Seller. If a property is sold at a higher price by virtue of agreeing to a cash incentive, the Seller who is a property investor may pay *more* capital gains tax if and when selling because the price *difference* will be that much more. Note that the capital gains amount is normally based on the difference between the buying price and the selling price as entered at the Land Registry. Hence, the *Cash Incentive* may ultimately have the effect of increasing the capital gains tax bill, assuming the Seller is liable for capital gains tax anyway. There are many ways to avoid or mitigate capital gains tax and therefore a Cash Incentive may have little or no effect. But remember that capital gains tax is not applicable if buying or selling your own home.

Important clarification regarding '*gifted deposits*':

- Do not confuse a *Cash Incentive*, as described in this book, with a so called '*gifted deposit*'. Nothing in this book makes use of a *gifted deposit*. In the past, *gifted deposits* were used as a means of getting an amount of money from a Lender that was *higher* than the selling price of the property. However, most Lenders no longer offer 'gifted deposit mortgages'.

- The strategies given in this book do not involve *gifted deposits*. Instead, a cash incentive is obtained from the Seller, a transaction that does not involve the Lender. Cash Incentives of this kind are perfectly legal and are widely used by house-building companies.

- A *Cash Incentive* is fundamentally different to a *gifted deposit* because (i) the lender is not involved in the cash incentive transaction, and (ii) the mortgage amount is based on the selling price only (with a *gifted deposit* the mortgage amount is based on the sum of the selling price PLUS the *gifted deposit* amount). A Lender is involved with a gifted deposit because the money for the gifted deposit is paid by the Lender to the Buyer, via the solicitor. It is important to make sure your solicitor understands the difference, and that you are not proposing to get involved with any kind of *gifted deposit.*

- Lenders are phasing out *gifted deposits* (even though they are legal) because 'mission creep' has set in. That is, the amount of the *gifted deposit* requested by borrowers (in addition to the loan amount to buy the property) was going up to 15%, 20%, and even 25% of the property value. As a result, some Buyers ended up taking on mortgage debts that they could not afford to repay. The tabloid press had a field day blaming Lenders for lending too much money to 'vulnerable' people.

- The *Cash Incentive* strategies proposed in this book are different because the Lenders are not involved in the process. The *Cash Incentive* is a private arrangement between the Buyer and the Seller (albeit through solicitors), and provided the mortgage is based on the SELLING PRICE and VALUATION, there can be no objections from any of the parties involved.

To reassure the Seller about this way of doing business, explain that virtually all house building companies operate this way. Show the Seller some typical advertisements, such as:

A. Advertisement extract from Kingsoak Homes: *'Options include 5% deposit paid, up to £10,000 cashback, stamp duty paid, home exchange, investor package'.*

B. Advertisement extract from Barratt Homes: *'Purchase plans include home exchange, 5% deposit paid, stamp duty paid, £5,000 cashback, investor package'.*

An examination of the Barratt's advertisement shows the following: Barratt is the Seller. So when a house is bought from Barratt, you the Buyer get a sum of money, i.e. a cash incentive. In this example, the cash incentive takes the form of a 5% deposit payment, a stamp duty payment, £5,000 in cash, and so on. In other words, Barratt is giving the Buyer a sum of money (financial package) as a reward for buying its property.

Note that Barratt has factored the cost of the cash incentive into its selling price, and that the Buyer will be getting a mortgage based on this selling price.

The Price Strategy For Buyers uses the same strategy employed by Barratt and many other property builders. In the example at the beginning of this chapter, the Seller is giving you, the Buyer, a £10,000 cash incentive in return for buying their property.

Thus when you apply *The Price Strategy For Buyers* you are, in effect, enabling the Seller to use the same selling methods used by large national builders. There is absolutely nothing underhand about this strategy – it is perfectly legal and proper. Private individuals have the same right to use this strategy as much as house-building companies do. So when you go to meet a Seller to negotiate a price, go equipped with advertisements from builders such as Barratt.

Note that if using a Cash Incentive to finance a mortgage deposit, a Buyer may have to obtain a bridging loan for two or three days (the time interval between paying the deposit to the solicitor to complete the deal and receiving the cash incentive to repay the bridging loan).

Make sure that you brief your solicitor about your intentions to ask for a 'cash incentive' in your negotiations, should this be necessary. Do this *before* you start to look for a property to buy. If your solicitor is not familiar with the concept of a cash incentive in a property transaction you should perhaps find another solicitor. Then, if a Seller needs reassurance about the strategy, you can tell the Seller to ask his solicitor to contact your solicitor to get confirmation that a *Cash Incentive* is a perfectly acceptable way of proceeding.

STEP 3: Confirm it in writing.

Let's recap. In step 1 you negotiated the best possible price without using any of the strategies in this book. In step 2 you made an offer based on *The Price Strategy For Buyers* and you got a positive response indicating co-operation with the strategy. Now, in step 3 you will be giving the Seller two letters.

The first letter is a written confirmation from you to the Seller to clarify the offer you have just made. This first letter would be issued in duplicate so that the Seller can sign and return one copy to indicate an agreement in principle to proceed.

The second letter is a draft letter for the Seller to send to his solicitor to get things moving. Both these letters are shown below, with suggested wording that can be adapted as necessary.

Note: these two letters would also be copied to any estate agent that may be involved in the transaction.

Written confirmation of offer from Buyer to Seller

(date)

From: (Buyer's name and address)

To: (Seller's name and address)

Re: Sale of your property (enter property address)

Following my viewing of your property, I would like to make a formal offer at the full asking price, made up as follows:

Full Offer Price:	£ (enter agreed price) [Note: In the case of the above example, this would be £210,000]
*Less Cash Incentive: (For redecoration, repairs, and miscellaneous costs)	£ (enter agreed amount) [Note: In the case of the above example, this would be £10,000]
Total cash on completion:	£ (enter difference of above two figures) [Note: In the case of the above example, this would be £200,000]

* The Cash Incentive referred to above is a sum of money that will be paid from the Seller's solicitor to the Buyer's solicitor on completion of the property transaction.

The address of my solicitor is as follows: (enter Buyer's solicitor details).

I confirm that I will declare the cash incentive on my mortgage application form. (Delete this paragraph if Buyer is not using a loan to buy the property).

This offer remains subject to satisfactory valuation and contract. The next step is to tell your solicitor to sell your property to me as explained above.

If an estate agent is involved, you need to ask the estate agent to issue a *'memorandum of sale'* and withdraw the property from the market. **Please ensure that your estate agent clearly understands that the SELLING PRICE is the amount before the Cash Incentive and not the 'discounted amount'.** The discounted amount must not appear on any documentation as it is not the agreed selling price. When I receive a copy of the *memorandum of sale* I will ask my Lender to carry out the mortgage valuation on the property.

Please sign the declaration below and give me a copy of this letter to indicate that you agree in principle to sell me your house on the terms given above.

If anything is not clear please contact me at any time.

Yours sincerely,

(enter Buyer's name)

DECLARATION BY SELLER: I agree in principle to sell you my property on the terms described above, subject to valuation and subject to contract.

Signed: .... Date:...........

Print Name: ....

You should give the Seller two copies of the above letter so that one copy can be signed and returned to you. You should then help the Seller further by giving him a draft letter for sending to his solicitor. Here is the wording:

56

Letter from Seller to Seller's solicitor

Dear (Solicitor)

Property: (Address)

I have asked you to act for me in the selling of my above property. I am writing to explain that I have found a buyer and the details are as follows:

1. Name of buyer: (enter name).

2. Buyer's solicitor: (enter name, address, and telephone number).

3. Price for selling property: (enter SELLING PRICE, not discounted amount).

4. Cash Incentive: I have also agreed to give the buyer a Cash Incentive of £ (enter amount). This sum of money is to be paid to the buyer or his solicitor upon completion, from the proceeds of sale. This means that the total cash on completion will be £xyz (the agreed price of £..... less the Cash Incentive of £.....).

    The Buyer will be declaring this Cash Incentive on his mortgage application form. (Delete this paragraph if the buyer is not borrowing money to buy the property.)

Please find enclosed a copy of the offer I have received from the buyer.

Yours sincerely

(name of Seller)

The above letter from the Seller to his solicitor is important as it will focus the Seller's mind into taking the correct action and being committed to following the strategy.

If the Seller will not sign the declaration in the letter there and then, you should allow the Seller to take the letter away, and consult their solicitor should they wish to. In this event, you should make it clear that you cannot commit to buying the property (and you will be looking at other properties) until the letter is signed or until you get a clear indication of an intention to sell the property to you.

Important Note: *When mentioning this strategy to a solicitor, only talk in terms of getting a Cash Incentive from the Seller. Do not talk in terms of getting a cashback from the Lender as this is not the case, and solicitors may regard this as somewhat dubious. Also, point out that you will be declaring the cash incentive on the mortgage application form, and that this is no different to getting a Cash Incentive from a house-building company, a practice that is common all over the UK.*

The Price Strategy For Buyers then, is using the *Lender's money* rather than your own money (assuming you have any!) to in effect, pay for stamp duty and other costs. In the above example it is much better to end up with a mortgage of £199,500 and have £10,000 cash-in-hand, than to end up with a mortgage of £190,000 and *no* cash-in-hand.

You may end up paying a little more in monthly interest on a mortgage of £199,500 compared to £190,000, but this difference is small. For example, if the mortgage interest is 5%, the monthly payment would be about £831 compared to £792 (a difference of about £39). Remember, you don't have to spend all of the Cash Incentive – you can if you wish, put some of the Cash Incentive money into a high-interest savings account to offset the small increase in monthly interest.

Or you could use any money remaining from the Cash Incentive to reduce your mortgage. You can even factor the Cash Incentive into the mortgage deposit, thereby reducing the amount you have to pay as a deposit. Another advantage is that you have £10,000 cash-in-hand (in this example) at a time when you most need it.

But the main advantage is that the £10,000 Cash Incentive has enabled the Buyer (in this example) to secure a house instead of losing it.

When buying your home with limited savings and limited income, a Cash Incentive can sometimes make or break a property deal. Remember: this is a *Cash Incentive* even though the money originates from the mortgage/loan money. If your <u>mortgage</u> also includes a Cash Incentive this is a ***mortgage cashback***, which is quite a different animal (see ***The Mortgage Cashback Strategy For Buyers*** in another chapter). Of course, there is nothing to stop you getting two cashbacks in the same deal: One from the Seller, and one from the Lender.

If you are running a buy-to-let business, ***The Price Strategy For Buyers*** will improve your cash flow and give you more equity. And the small increase in monthly interest will not matter as much since you get tax relief on rental income.

No Price Reduction

We have seen that the amount of the Cash Incentive relates directly to the amount of the price reduction that can be negotiated. In our example the price reduction was £10,000 and hence the Cash Incentive was £10,000. But what happens when no price reduction is available?

In this scenario, the Buyer must decide whether he still wants to buy the property even though the Seller will not agree to any price reduction. If so, ***The Price Strategy For Buyers*** can still be used to good effect and this is how it works.

- The objective is to buy the property without having to pay for stamp duty out of your own resources. The solution is to get the Lender (the mortgage company) to pay for the stamp duty. But Lenders will not do this because they normally only lend money for the cost of the actual property.

- The way round this is to ask the Seller to increase the SELLING PRICE by an amount equivalent to (or a bit more than) the stamp duty, rounded off to the nearest one hundred pounds. The Buyer would then get a mortgage based on this higher price.

- For example, if the asking price is £210,000 and no price reduction is possible, the Buyer would ask the Seller to increase the price to, say, £213,000. This would be the agreed SELLING PRICE on *all* relevant documents.

- The Buyer would also ask the Seller for a £3,000 Cash Incentive, using the same negotiating strategy described in this chapter. The net result is that the Seller gets the asking price of £210,000, and the Buyer gets a mortgage based on £213,000 plus £3,000 cash in hand.

- Note that in the negotiating strategy described in this chapter it is suggested that the Buyer give the Seller £300 by buying some chattels. However, the amount of £300 is not set in stone; this could, for example, be reduced to £100.

- This strategy is perfectly legal and proper since the tax authorities will be getting even more stamp duty than otherwise. Furthermore, nobody has been misled, and provided the mortgage valuation is not lower than the SELLING PRICE of £213,000 the Lender will be happy.

Note that you can combine both scenarios: if you get a small price reduction of, say, £500, you could ask for a Cash Incentive of £3,500 (the difference between the SELLING PRICE of £213,000 and the £209,500 to be paid for the property). In this scenario, each party would tell their solicitors that the SELLING PRICE is £213,000 and the Cash Incentive is £3,500.

In fact, in most property transactions it will be a matter of combining two amounts and getting a Cash Incentive for the total. These two amounts will be: (i) the difference between the asking price and the reduced price negotiated, and (ii) the difference between the asking price and a higher price based on adding the stamp duty.

To clarify this further, here is an example:

1. The asking price is £210,000.

2. **Discount amount £5,000.** After negotiation a price reduction of £5,000 is on offer, bringing the price down to £205,000.

3. **Stamp duty amount £2,000.** The stamp duty on £210,000 at 1% is £2,100, so the Seller is asked to increase the selling price by, say £2,000 (from £210,000 to £212,000).

4. The Seller is asked for a Cash Incentive of £7,000 (the total of the discount amount of £5,000 and the stamp duty amount of £2,000).

5. The Seller gets paid the agreed £205,000 and the Buyer gets a mortgage based on £212,000 with a Cash Incentive of £7,000.

When the two elements (the discount amount and the stamp duty amount) are combined, this is a very powerful and effective strategy.

Summary of *The Price Strategy For Buyers:*

1. Brief your solicitor about the use of a 'Cash Incentive' for buying your next property. Say that you will be asking the Seller to give you a small Cash Incentive upon completion. Should you need to explain further, go through the example at the beginning of this chapter. You should not need to explain the whole strategy. If the solicitor is not familiar with the concept of a Cash Incentive find another. The purpose here is to 'prime' your solicitor to be receptive. and to fully co-operate with the Seller's solicitor when the time comes. Any experienced conveyancer will be familiar with the concept of a Cash Incentive.

2. Find a property and negotiate the best price reduction possible. Use *The Price Strategy For Buyers*, whether or not a price reduction can be obtained. If a price reduction is granted, ask the Seller for a Cash Incentive equivalent to the price reduction. If no price reduction is granted, ask the Seller for a Cash Incentive equivalent to the amount of stamp duty (you do this by asking the Seller to increase the SELLING PRICE by an amount equivalent to the stamp duty).

3. Offer the Seller an additional £300 (or some other amount) to encourage his cooperation. Do this by offering to buy a low value item (or items) in the property for £300, and say this will be a separate cash transaction between you and the Seller.

4. Show the Seller one or more advertisements used by building companies such as Barratt, offering Cash Incentives in the form of money, **stamp duty payments**, and so on. Explain that what you are proposing is no different to the way that large building companies operate, but on a smaller scale. Explain that a Cash Incentive is a perfectly legal and common way of doing business.

5. Make full use of a combined strategy to get as big a Cash Incentive as possible. Do this by combining the discount amount with the stamp duty amount. That way you will always get a Cash Incentive, even when little or no price reduction can be obtained.

6. Tell Seller the next step is to inform their solicitor (and estate agent if applicable). Do this by using the two sample letters given above.

7. Follow through with all parties (Seller, Estate Agent, Solicitor, Lender) to get things moving.

The Valuation Strategy For Buyers

The Valuation Strategy For Buyers is one of the best ways of saving stamp duty costs and other property purchase costs. It's a 'win, win' situation for all concerned, and as you will see, a strategy that should be applied to virtually all property purchases.

This strategy is based on the principle of getting a full market valuation for the property (the higher the valuation the better). A good (i.e. high) valuation will result in a more favourable loan, increased equity, higher profits, and better cash flow. Let's briefly look at the financial elements that go into this strategy.

PRICE (or SELLING PRICE). Normally, when a PRICE is agreed between Buyer and Seller, this is the figure that goes on your mortgage application form. And provided that the valuation carried out by the LENDER is not *less* than the PRICE, you will get a mortgage based on this figure.

AMOUNT PAID. This is the reduced price that has been negotiated and agreed upon, and is the actual amount of money that the Seller will end up getting for the property. Note that the LOAN is based on the PRICE (not the AMOUNT PAID), provided the VALUATION is not lower than the PRICE.

VALUATION. This is the open market value deemed to apply to the property by the LENDER. So here we are not talking about a valuation carried out by an estate agent or anybody else (unless employed by the LENDER to do the valuation). Rather, it is based on the resell value and not the cost of rebuilding. Should the property be repossessed, the LENDER wants evidence that money will be recouped by reselling the property.

LENDER. The mortgage company or bank that is lending money to the buyer as a secured loan, i.e. the loan is secured on the property.

COMPARABLE. This stands for 'comparable price'. It refers to another property near the one you want to buy (same postal district or within one to two miles), that is similar in type and price. So if you have three comparables, it means you have information on three other properties that can be compared to the property you are buying or selling in terms of price and type of property. Comparables do not have to be physically identical to the property being sold, just roughly similar, so that like is compared with like.

Coming back to the VALUATION, the sequence of events leading up to the valuation is as follows:

1. Find a property you want to buy.
2. Agree a price.
3. Seller and Buyer both instruct solicitors.
4. Buyer applies for a mortgage.
5. Lender carries out a valuation and if satisfactory (i.e. not lower than the PRICE) a mortgage is granted.

The *Valuation Strategy For Buyers* involves getting as high a valuation as possible in order to fully reflect the open market value of the property. This is perfectly legal and proper, as no misrepresentation of the value is involved.

The following example explains the strategy further:

EXAMPLE

- Seller's asking price: £230,000

- Rock bottom amount that Seller is willing to accept after negotiation: £228,000

- For this example we assume a valuation of £238,000

- Buyer can get a 95% Loan to Value mortgage. Deposit is therefore 5%

In this example we will compare two scenarios:

Scenario one, based on the *traditional approach*

1. Original asking price: £230,000
2. Amount paid (price agreed after negotiation): £228,000.
3. Agreed selling price: £228,000.
4. Mortgage amount is £216,600 (95% of £228,000).
5. Mortgage Deposit (payment from Buyer to Buyer's Lender): £11,400 (5% of £228,000).

6. Buyer has to pay stamp duty, legal fees, mortgage valuation, and all other costs out of own resources as these cannot be included in the mortgage loan.

7. Property is registered at the land registry with a value of £228,000.

Scenario two based on *The Valuation Strategy For Buyers*

1. Original asking price: £230,000

2. Amount paid (price agreed after negotiation): £228,000.

3. Agreed selling price: £238,000 (£10,000 more than the amount to be paid after negotiating a price reduction).

4. Cash Incentive agreed (payment from Seller to Buyer): £10,000 (difference between £238,000 and £228,000, thereby Seller gets £228,000 for house).

5. Mortgage amount is £226,100 (95% of £238,000).

6. Mortgage Deposit (payment from Buyer to Buyer's Lender): £11,900 (5% of £238,000).

7. Buyer can pay stamp duty, legal fees, mortgage valuation, and all other costs from the £10,000 Cash Incentive, and still have money left over.

8. Property is registered at the land registry with a value of £238,000.

We will now look at scenario two in more detail and explain the strategy further. What follows is a step-by-step procedure, including suggested dialogue. There are three steps to follow.

STEP 1: Negotiate a price.

STEP 2: Make an offer.

STEP 3: Confirm it in writing.

STEP 1: Negotiate a price.

The Buyer and Seller will negotiate a price in the usual manner. It is assumed in this example that a price reduction of £2,000 has been agreed, making the amount to pay £228,000. Note, however, that *The Valuation Strategy For Buyers* can be used even where no price reduction is forthcoming, or where there is a price gap to bridge.

STEP 2: Make an offer.

The Seller may think that negotiations are over, but for the Buyer this is where the negotiations start and *The Valuation Strategy For Buyers* now springs into action.

Having clearly agreed a price reduction to £228,000, you now ask the Seller to agree a SELLING PRICE of £238,000. This apparent *volte-face* may come as a surprise to the Seller, but the Buyer goes on to explain that the price to be paid will still only be £228,000. The dialogue would go along the lines that follow.

Note: Speak slowly when negotiating, don't rush things through. Also, pause after each 'chunk' of dialogue to make sure the Seller has heard you correctly, and make certain there are no misunderstandings. If you get any questions and you don't want to stop at that point, say *'I will go on to explain that in just a moment'.*

Dialogue:

- *'Now that we've agreed a price of £228,000 this is the amount I will be paying you. I like your house very much and it shouldn't be devalued. I want to enter the full market value at the Land Registry. Therefore I want to ask you to agree a selling price of £238,000. I also want to ask you to give me a Cash Incentive of £10,000. This means you get the agreed £228,000, but the house value will go through on the Land Registry as £238,000.'*

  Note: You will have arrived at a figure of £238,000 having researched the values of similar properties in the area (more on this later).

- *'The house price of £238,000 is the price that would go on all the paperwork including my mortgage application. This will help me cover legal fees, stamp duty, and other costs such as certain renovation work before I move in.'*

- *'This method of buying your house won't affect you in any way. On completion, my solicitor will give your solicitor the agreed selling price of £238,000. Your solicitor will then give my solicitor the £10,000 Cash Incentive. Of course, you will need to tell your solicitor about this so I will give you a letter that explains everything.*

- *'All that we have discussed is completely legal and above board, and is common practice throughout the building industry. The £10,000 price difference is called a 'Cash Incentive', and any experienced conveyancer will be familiar with this way of doing business. This £10,000 is a Cash Incentive from you to me, but the money does not come from you – it comes from the money I am borrowing to buy your house.'*

- *'The Cash Incentive is, in effect, a payment from my Lender to me, but it goes through you. Have a look at this diagram.'* (see next page)

FIG. 7 - MONEY-FLOW DIAGRAM

Step 1

LENDER

(Money loaned to Buyer, based on selling price)

Step 2

BUYER'S SOLICITOR

(Money given to Buyer's solicitor for buying property)

Step 3

SELLER'S SOLICITOR

(Money paid to Seller's solicitor on completion, without deducting the Cash Incentive)

Step 4

BUYER'S SOLICITOR

(Seller's solicitor 'pays' Cash Incentive money to Buyer's solicitor for giving to Buyer)

Step 5

BUYER

Buyer receives Cash Incentive money as part of the final reconciliation of the completion statement prepared by the Buyer's solicitor

---

To finish this point, explain that the Cash Incentive amounts to surplus money left over from the mortgage loan (the difference between the amount borrowed and the amount actually paid for the property). You now continue the dialogue to finish the negotiations.

- *'Have a look at these advertisements. What I am proposing is no different to the way that large building companies operate. You and I are doing the same thing but on a smaller scale. In these advertisements, the building companies are selling direct to buyers, just as you are selling direct to me.'*
  (Show advertisements depicting Cash Incentive offers from builders like Barratt. Answer any remaining questions).

- *'If you can help me out by doing this I will be very pleased to buy your (fridge/curtains/sofa/flower pots/whatever) for £300. I will pay you cash for these items as a separate transaction. So you will end up getting the £228,000 payment for the house, and in addition you get a separate cash payment direct from me for £300.'*

Make sure that you have established beforehand in your own mind which item (or items) you will be buying for £300. It needs to be an item of little value, or an item that would have been included in the price of the house anyway. That way, the £300 will be genuinely appreciated.

- *'If you will agree to this method of selling your property this is how you will benefit:*

  1. *You get to sell your property at the agreed price.*

  2. *You can stop looking for a buyer as you will now be able to sell your property. It means you can move on with other things in your life, knowing that you have sold this house.*

  3. *Your property will not be devalued in the local market place as it will be registered at the higher value of £238,000. This can benefit you or your relatives who may own other properties in the area.*

  4. *You get an additional £300 as a separate cash payment direct from me.'*

(Give the Seller a separate sheet showing these four benefits).

- *'So can I take it that you agree in principle with this strategy? If so, I will give you a letter confirming my agreement to buy your house. I will also give you a letter that you can send to your solicitor which explains the strategy we have been talking about.'*

Stop to make sure the Seller has heard you correctly, and make certain there are no misunderstandings. At this point you must wait to get an answer to know whether or not the Seller is going to co-operate. Do not proceed to STEP 3 if it is clear that the Seller will not cooperate.

The benefits to the Seller are:

1. Seller has found a Buyer and can sell the house.

2. Seller gets a bonus, e.g. £300.

3. Seller's house is not devalued in the local market place (this can benefit the Seller if he owns other local properties, or has nearby relatives who own properties).

The benefits to the Buyer are:

1. Buyer gets a property at below market value (a good bargain).

2. Buyer gets a property with equity, i.e. the potential profit that can be made when re-selling the property.

3. Buyer gets cash (in this example £10,000 less £300) that can be used to pay for stamp duty, legal fees, conveyancing costs, or just be put into a savings account!).

TIP

Prepare a sheet of paper that just shows the four Buyer benefits. Use a large size font and use the word 'you' instead of 'Buyer'. Give this sheet to the Buyer when you mention these benefits.

The key to *The Valuation Strategy For Buyers* is the price difference between the 'official' price on which the mortgage is based, and the actual amount paid to the Seller. This difference is the *cash incentive*. In the building industry it is common for house builders to offer cash incentives, and the amount of the cash incentive will have been factored into the selling price. Hence, there is no legal difference between a cash incentive offered by a house builder and a cash incentive offered by a private individual as described in this strategy.

Provided the cash incentive is not more than 10% of the PRICE it will usually not be a cause for concern to anybody. If it is not over 5% (as in this example) it should be perfectly acceptable to all parties. However, cash incentives of 15% are not uncommon in the building industry.

Note: The Buyer may declare the *Cash Incentive* on his mortgage application form (there is nothing to hide). The Lender will not mind that the Buyer is getting a Cash Incentive provided the selling price is in line with the valuation report. Remember three things: (i) The *Cash Incentive* is not an additional loan from the Lender, (ii) the Lender is not involved with the Cash Incentive in any direct or legal sense, and (iii) Lenders themselves give Cash Incentives to Buyers (just look at any mortgage magazine).

A Cash Incentive received by a Buyer is not usually regarded as income and is therefore tax free. This is so because the amount is relatively small and is not part of an estate being inherited. The cashback is akin to a gift – if you receive a gift of money it is tax free, like winning the lottery! The only exception to this is a professional property trader/investor. If you are in the business of buying and selling property for a living, then the *Cash Incentive* is regarded as income or profit and is therefore taxable, just like any other earned income. If a *Cash Incentive* is received by a Company, but not a property trading company, it may be taxable depending on the financial situation of the Company, and advice from a tax accountant may be appropriate.

Regarding Capital Gains Tax, this will not apply if buying or selling your own home (the place where you live). If the property is bought or sold by a property trader/investor, e.g. for reselling or for buy-to-let, the following applies:

Buyer. If a property is bought at a higher price by virtue of getting a Cash Incentive, the Buyer who is a property investor will pay *less* capital gains tax if and when selling because the price *difference* will be that much less. Note that the capital gains amount is normally based on the difference between the buying price and the selling price as entered at the Land Registry. Hence, the *Cash Incentive* will ultimately have the effect of reducing the capital gains tax bill. But remember that capital gains tax is not applicable if buying or selling your own home.

Seller. If a property is sold at a higher price by virtue of agreeing to a Cash Incentive, the Seller who is a property investor may pay *more* capital gains tax if and when selling because the price *difference* will be that much more. Note that the capital gains amount is normally based on the difference between the buying price and the selling price as entered at the Land Registry. Hence, the *Cash Incentive* may ultimately have the effect of increasing the capital gains tax bill, assuming the Seller is liable for capital gains tax anyway. There are many ways to avoid or mitigate capital gains tax and therefore a Cash Incentive may have little or no effect. But remember that capital gains tax is not applicable if buying or selling your own home.

Important clarification regarding *'gifted deposits'*:

- Do not confuse a *Cash Incentive*, as described in this book, with a so called *'gifted deposit'*. Nothing in this book makes use of a *gifted deposit*. In the past, *gifted deposits* were used as a means of getting an amount of money from a Lender that was *higher* than the selling price of the property. However, most Lenders no longer offer 'gifted deposit mortgages'.

- The strategies given in this book do not involve *gifted deposits*. Instead, a *Cash Incentive* is obtained from the Seller, a transaction that does not involve the Lender. Cash Incentives of this kind are perfectly legal and are widely used by house-building companies.

- A *Cash Incentive* is fundamentally different to a *gifted deposit* because (i) the lender is not involved in the Cash Incentive transaction, and (ii) the mortgage amount is based on the selling price only (with a *gifted deposit* the mortgage amount is based on the sum of the selling price PLUS the *gifted deposit* amount). A Lender is involved with a gifted deposit because the money for the gifted deposit is paid by the Lender to the Buyer, via the solicitor. It is important to make sure your solicitor understands the difference, and that you are not proposing to get involved with any kind of *gifted deposit*.

- Lenders are phasing out *gifted deposits* (even though they are legal) because 'mission creep' has set in. That is, the amount of the *gifted deposit* requested by borrowers (in addition to the loan amount to buy the property) was going up to 15%, 20%, and even 25% of the property value. As a result, some Buyers ended up taking on mortgage debts that they could not afford to repay. The tabloid press had a field day blaming Lenders for lending too much money to 'vulnerable' people.

- The *Cash Incentive* strategies proposed in this book are different because the Lenders are not involved in the process. The *Cash Incentive* is a private arrangement between the Buyer and the Seller (albeit through solicitors), and provided the mortgage is based on the SELLING PRICE and VALUATION, there can be no objections from any of the parties involved.

To reassure the Seller about this way of doing business, explain that virtually all house building companies operate this way. Show the Seller some typical advertisements such as the following:

A. Advertisement extract from Kingsoak Homes: *'Options include 5% deposit paid, up to £10,000 cashback, stamp duty paid, home exchange, investor package'.*

B. Advertisement extract from Barratt Homes: *'Purchase plans include home exchange, 5% deposit paid, stamp duty paid, £5,000 cashback, investor package'.*

An examination of the Barratt advertisement shows the following: Barratt is the Seller. So when a house is bought from Barratt, the Buyer gets a sum of money, i.e. a Cash Incentive. In this example, the Cash Incentive takes the form of a 5% deposit payment, a **stamp duty** payment, £5,000 cash, and so on. In other words, Barratt is giving the Buyer a sum of money (financial package) as a reward for buying its property.

Note that Barratt has factored the cost of the Cash Incentive into its selling price, and that the Buyer will be getting a mortgage based on this selling price.

The Valuation Strategy For Buyers uses the same strategy employed by Barratt and many other property builders. In the example at the beginning of this chapter, the Seller is giving you, the Buyer, a £10,000 Cash Incentive in return for buying their property.

Thus when you apply *The Valuation Strategy For Buyers* you are, in effect, enabling the Seller to use the same selling methods used by large national builders. There is absolutely nothing underhand about this strategy – it is perfectly legal and proper. Private individuals have the same right to use this strategy as much as house-building companies do. So when you go to meet a Seller to negotiate a price, go equipped with advertisements from builders such as Barratt.

Note that if using a Cash Incentive to finance a mortgage deposit, a Buyer may have to obtain a bridging loan for two or three days (the time interval between paying the deposit to the solicitor to complete the deal and receiving the Cash Incentive to repay the bridging loan).

Make sure that you brief your solicitor about your plan to ask a Buyer for a *Cash Incentive* if you cannot get the price you want. Do this *before* you start to look for a property to buy. If your solicitor is not familiar with the concept of a *Cash Incentive* in a property transaction you should perhaps find another solicitor. Then, if a Seller needs reassurance about the strategy, you can tell the Seller to ask his solicitor to contact your solicitor to get confirmation that the *Cash Incentive* is a perfectly acceptable way of proceeding.

STEP 3: Confirm it in writing.

Let's recap. In step 1 you negotiated the best possible price in the conventional manner. In step 2 you made an offer based on *The Valuation Strategy for Buyers* and you got a positive response indicating cooperation with the strategy. Now, in step 3 you will be giving the Seller two letters.

The first letter is a written confirmation from you to the Seller to clarify the offer you have just made. This first letter would be issued in duplicate so that the Seller can sign and return one copy to indicate an agreement in principle to proceed.

The second letter is a draft letter for the Seller to send to his solicitor to get things moving. Both these letters are shown below, with suggested wording that can be adapted as necessary.

Written confirmation of offer from Buyer to Seller

(date)

From: (Buyer's name and address)

To: (Seller's name and address)

Re: Sale of your property (enter property address)

Following my viewing of your property, I would like to make a formal offer made up as follows (See next page):

Full Offer Price:	£ (enter agreed price) [Note: In the case of our example, this would be £238,000]
*Less Cash Incentive: (For redecoration, repairs, and miscellaneous costs)	£ (enter agreed amount) [Note: In the case of our example, this would be £10,000]
Total cash on completion:	£ (enter difference of above two figures) [Note: In the case of the our example, this would be £228,000]

*The Cash Incentive referred to above is a sum of money that will be paid from the Seller's solicitor to the Buyer's solicitor on completion of the property transaction.

The address of my solicitor is as follows: (enter Buyer's solicitor details).

I confirm that I will declare the Cash Incentive on my mortgage application form. (Delete this paragraph if Buyer is not using a loan to buy the property).

This offer is subject to satisfactory valuation and contract. The next step is to tell your solicitor to sell your property to me as explained above.

If an estate agent is involved, you need to ask the estate agent to issue a '*memorandum of sale*' and withdraw the property from the market. **Please ensure that your estate agent clearly understands that the SELLING PRICE is the amount before the Cash Incentive and not the discounted amount.** When I receive a copy of the *memorandum of sale* I will ask my Lender to carry out the mortgage valuation on the property.

Please sign the declaration below and give me a copy of this letter to indicate that you agree in principle to sell me your house on the terms given above.

If anything is not clear please contact me at any time.

Yours sincerely,

(enter Buyer's name)

DECLARATION BY SELLER: I agree to sell you my property on the terms described above, subject to valuation and subject to contract.

Signed:.....................................Date:...........

Print Name: ....

In addition to giving the Seller the above letter to confirm your offer, you should also make his job easy by giving him a draft letter for sending to his solicitor. Here is the wording:

Letter from Seller to Seller's solicitor

Dear (Solicitor)

Property: (Address)

I have asked you to act for me in the selling of my above property. I am writing to explain that I have found a buyer and the details are as follows:

1. Name of buyer: (enter name).

2. Buyer's solicitor: (enter name, address, and telephone number).

3. Price for selling property: (enter SELLING PRICE, not discounted amount).

4. Cash Incentive: I have also agreed to give the buyer a Cash Incentive of £ (enter amount). This sum of money is to be paid to the buyer upon completion, from the proceeds of sale. This means that the total cash on completion will be £xyz (the agreed price of £..... less the Cash Incentive of £.....).

Please find enclosed a copy of the offer I have received from the buyer.

Yours sincerely

(name of Seller)

The above letter from the Seller to his solicitor is important as it will focus the Seller's mind into taking the correct action and being committed to following the strategy.

If the Seller will not sign the declaration in the letter there and then, you should allow the Seller to consult his solicitor should he wish to. In this event, you the Buyer should make it clear that you cannot commit to buying the property, or stop looking at other properties, until the letter is signed or until you get a clear indication of an intention to sell the property to you.

Important Note: *When mentioning this strategy to a solicitor, only talk in terms of getting a Cash Incentive from the Seller. Do not talk in terms of getting a cashback from the Lender as this is not the case, and solicitors may regard this as somewhat dubious. Also, point out that you will be declaring the cash incentive on the mortgage application form, and that this is no different to getting a Cash Incentive from a house-building company, a practice that is common all over the UK.*

The Valuation Strategy For Buyers then, is using the *Lender's money* rather than your own money (assuming you have any!) to pay for stamp duty and other costs. In the above example it is much better to end up with a mortgage of £226,100, and have £10,000 cash-in-hand, than to end up with a mortgage of £216,600, and no cash-in-hand.

You may end up paying a little more in monthly interest on a mortgage of £226,100 compared to £216,600, but the difference is negligible. For example, if the mortgage interest is 5%, the monthly payment would be about £942 compared to £903 (a difference of about £39). Remember, you don't have to spend all of the Cash Incentive – you can if you want put some of the Cash Incentive money into a high-interest savings account to offset the small increase in monthly interest.

Or if you wanted to, you could use any money remaining from the Cash Incentive to reduce your mortgage. You can even factor the Cash Incentive into the mortgage deposit, thus reducing the amount you have to pay as a deposit. The main advantage is that you have £10,000 cash-in-hand (in this example) at a time when you most need it.

When buying a home with limited savings and limited income, a Cash Incentive from the Seller can sometimes make or break a property deal. Remember: this is a *Cash Incentive,* not a *Mortgage Cashback.* If the mortgage company itself is providing a cashback you get two cashbacks! One from the Seller, and one from the Lender.

If you are running a buy-to-let business, *The Valuation Strategy For Buyers* will improve your cash flow and give you more equity. And the small increase in monthly interest will not matter as much since you get tax relief on rental income.

The Big Question

We now come to the question of how best to get a full market valuation? In the above example, a valuation of £238,000 is needed for this strategy to work. If the valuation carried out by the Lender is different to the PRICE what will happen?

If the VALUATION is less than the PRICE, the Lender will either say NO to the LOAN, or offer a reduced LOAN based on the lower VALUATION.

If the VALUATION is the same as, or higher than the PRICE, the Lender will grant the LOAN applied for. Note that the Valuer will usually try to make the valuation match the PRICE, knowing that this is most advantageous to both the Lender and the Buyer.

When you apply for a mortgage you will be stating the PRICE on the application form, e.g. £238,000. The Lender then instructs a local estate agent or Valuation company to carry out a valuation. Note that although you, the Buyer, are paying for the valuation, the Valuer is working for the Lender and reports back to the Lender.

So how do you make sure that you get the VALUATION that you need? This is how:

Step one: check out local property prices

- Before you make an offer on the property, and before you negotiate a reduction, find out the approximate values of similar properties in the area. Do this by enquiring at local estate agents, by checking local property newspapers, and by walking or driving around the area looking for other properties for sale or sold. Finding COMPARABLES is at the heart of the strategy.

- If this initial research reveals several more highly priced
  properties that could be COMPARABLES, you know you
  may be able to apply *The Valuation Strategy For Buyers*. If
  you find that there are no similar properties at higher
  prices and if you feel that the target property is not
  undervalued, you should consider not applying *The
  Valuation Strategy For Buyers*. If you find that comparable
  prices are *lower* rather than higher, use this information to
  negotiate a lower price and apply *The Price Strategy For
  Buyers* instead. Either way, your time will not be wasted.

Step two: Use the Internet to get comparables

- Get property prices for the particular postcode by using the
  Internet. Simply go to:
  http://www.landreg.gov.uk/propertyprice/interactive/ppr_u
  albs.asp.
  Then enter a postcode and you will immediately get details
  of the average price of different types of properties. For
  example, if you are buying a flat in postcode RG1 7NT, you
  will see that in the last three months 43 flats were sold in
  this postcode, and the average price was £149,881. This is
  a **free service**. You can also get this information by phone
  or email but you will be charged £10 (Telephone
  01514736008, **Email:** enquiries.pic@landregistry.gov.uk).

- Why is this information useful? Because if prices for
  similar properties are higher you know you will be able to
  find some good comparables. If prices for similar
  properties are lower, you may have to reconsider *The
  Valuation Strategy For Buyers* and instead apply *The Price
  Strategy For Buyers*.

80

- Get comparables from *Home Track* on the Internet. Go to **http://www.hometrack.co.uk** (Tel 0800 019 4440) where you will be able to get a detailed market report for properties in any given postcode. The cost is about £15, and for that you get in-depth analysis of property, prices and trends, all focused on a particular postcode. You also get a list of nearby comparables and their locations, shown by dots on a street map. So although you don't get the actual addresses of comparables, there is enough information for you to be able to go there and see the property and the address. Naturally, you should be focused on the comparables with the highest values, and begin to compile a shortlist of three or four for giving to the Valuer.

- Once you have a few comparables, you may want to know the details of specific comparables. For instance, you may want to know the name of the owner, the actual price paid, the name of the Lender, and so on. To get this kind of information you can either knock on the front door and make enquiries, or you can get this information from the Land Registry. For a fee of just £2 you can get a copy of the Land Registry Entry for any given property in the UK, showing the legal history, price and date sold, full names of owners, etc. You can do this online over the internet by going to: **www.landregisteronline.gov.uk** and following the prompts to buy online.

Alternatively contact the Land Registry:
Telephone 0151 4736008
Fax 0151 4710151
Email: enquiries.pic@landregistry.gov.uk.

This is worth doing for the shortlist of two or three comparables that you will be giving to the Valuer – by giving the Valuer the full works (i.e. copies of the Land Registry entries) he won't have to double check the veracity of the information and he will be more inclined to go by the prices you give him.

Step three: Meet Valuer at property

- Make sure that you arrange to meet the Valuer at the property when he goes along to do the valuation. *This is critical. There is no other way of giving him the comparables.* Do this by stating on your mortgage application form that the Valuer *must make an appointment with you, the Buyer,* to gain access to the property. Then, when the Valuer contacts you to make an appointment, agree a date and time and make sure there will be no problems with the house occupants and gaining access on the day.

- Meet the Valuer at the property (be polite and friendly). Walk around with the Valuer, and offer to help in any way.

Tip

During the valuation do anything you can to help the Valuer: Make his job easy by giving him Land Registry entries for the highest value comparables. Ideally three comparables are required.

- Give The Valuer the comparables that you have prepared beforehand, and say *'to help you save time I have obtained some comparables which you can take with you'.* Remember two things: (i) The Valuer is working for the *Lender,* not for you, and (ii) he will use the PRICE given to him *by the Lender and by you* as a guide for arriving at a valuation figure. The Valuer will be trying hard to give a value that is equal to the PRICE rather than some other figure, provided the COMPARABLES stack up.

Summary of *The Valuation Strategy For Buyers:*

1. Brief your solicitor about the use of a 'Cash Incentive' to buy your next property. Say that you will be asking the Seller to give you a small Cash Incentive upon completion. Should you need to explain further, go through the two scenarios in the above example. You should not need to explain the whole strategy. If the solicitor is not familiar with the concept of a cash incentive in a property transaction find another solicitor. The purpose here is to 'prime' your solicitor to be receptive and to fully co-operate with the Seller's solicitor when the time comes. Any experienced conveyancer will be familiar with the concept of a Cash Incentive.

2. Find a property and negotiate the best price reduction possible. Having clearly ascertained the lowest price you can get, go on to ask the Seller to sell the house to you at the full value price. Explain that the difference between the full value price and the negotiated price represents the Cash Incentive that you will get. Since the Seller is not financially affected, there should be no objections.

3. Offer the Seller an additional £300 (or some other amount) to encourage cooperation. Do this by offering to buy a low value item in the property for £300, and say this will be a separate cash transaction between you and the Seller.

4. Show the Seller one or more advertisements used by building companies such as Barratt, who offer Cash Incentives in the form **stamp duty payments**, and so on. Explain that what you are proposing is no different to the way that large building companies operate, but on a smaller scale. Explain that a Cash Incentive in the building industry is a perfectly legal and common way of doing business.

5. Tell Seller the next step is to inform their solicitor (and estate agent if applicable). Do this by using the sample letters given.

6. Make sure you enter the agreed full market value PRICE on the mortgage application form, and clearly state that the Valuer must contact you personally to arrange to see the property for the VALUATION (do not give alternative contact details for the Valuer). It is crucial that you are able to meet the Valuer at the property because this is the only opportunity you have for giving him the COMPARABLES.

7. Find out the highest value comparables in the area by doing research in the locality and on the Internet, and prepare a shortlist of two or three comparables for giving to the Valuer (as a rule the Valuer needs three comparables).

8. Follow through with all parties (Seller, Estate Agent, Solicitor, Lender) to get things moving.

The Combination Strategy For Buyers

So far we have looked at the following six strategies:

1	**The Tax Exemption Strategy For Buyers**
2	**The Threshold Strategy For Buyers**
3	**The Link Strategy For Buyers**
4	**The Mortgage Cashback Strategy For Buyers**
5	**The Price Strategy For Buyers**
6	**The Valuation Strategy For Buyers**

The Combination Strategy For Buyers is a way of exploiting any 'mix and match' of these six strategies to give a powerful and infallible way of avoiding, reducing or saving the cost of stamp duty.

Every time you buy a property you will be using a different mix of these strategies, depending on the circumstances. Furthermore, it is unlikely that you will be using just one of these strategies whenever buying a property.

So let's look at how you can combine these strategies and make the best savings possible. Clearly, you need to understand the six strategies by reading the preceding pages before continuing with this chapter.

The Tax Exemption Strategy For Buyers, based on getting tax relief in disadvantaged areas, is a clear-cut situation: it either applies or does not apply. If it does apply, then it would be used in conjunction with other strategies in this book.

The Threshold Strategy For Buyers, based on exploiting stamp duty thresholds and negotiating lower property prices, should always be considered if the asking PRICE is near to or within the price threshold. For example, if the property is priced at, say, £269,000 you know that the price has not been reduced to get under any particular threshold. In these circumstances you would dismiss *The Threshold Strategy For Buyers* and consider another strategy.

However, if the property is priced at, say, £259,000 or £262,000 you know that either A or B is a possibility:

A. The owner considered the property was worth around, say, £255,000, but as this is too close to the stamp duty threshold it wouldn't attract buyers. Therefore, in order to attract buyers the price was changed upwards to £259,000. This gives room for negotiation.

B. The owner considered the property was worth around, say, £255,000, but as this is too close to the stamp duty threshold it wouldn't attract buyers. Therefore, in order to attract buyers the price was changed downwards to £250,000. This will stop buyers being put off by the stamp duty threshold (the jump from 1% to 3%), but clearly the price is unlikely to be reduced further.

So *The Threshold Strategy For Buyers* is a pretty clear cut situation: it either applies or it's a non-starter (you won't know until you negotiate). If there is a possibility the strategy may apply (because the price is near the threshold) see what other strategies in this book it can be combined *before* you approach the Seller.

The Link Strategy For Buyers, based on avoiding a punitive rate of stamp duty when buying more than one property from the same Seller, can be combined with just about any other strategy in this book. You would, of course, only consider using this strategy if there was a possibility of buying a property from a Seller that has already sold you a property in the past (or if buying two or more properties from anybody).

Looking at other strategies, you could get a £1,000 cashback mortgage from a Lender using *The Mortgage Cashback Strategy For Buyers,* and on top of that you could get a £3,000 Cash Incentive from the Seller based on *The Valuation Strategy For Buyers.* So, in this example you have combined several stamp avoidance strategies to give you a big saving in stamp duty, plus £4,000 in cash.

The point is this: whatever property deal you may be orchestrating, exploit all six strategies in whichever ways are possible. Some property deals may warrant all six strategies! Others may just warrant one of the strategies. Most property deals will be amenable to at least two of the strategies. It would be very unusual to buy a property without being able to apply at least one of the stamp duty avoidance strategies in this book.

The Mortgage Cashback Strategy For Buyers, based on getting a cashback from the Lender, is great provided you are not sacrificing some other useful feature of the mortgage package. This strategy would be used in conjunction with any other strategy that may apply, to give you additional funds for paying **stamp duty** and other costs. Do not dismiss this strategy just because you are also getting a Cash Incentive from the Seller or mortgage broker. Get as many Cash Incentives as you can, from all directions!

We now come to the ideal *combination strategy method* to give a virtually foolproof way of saving money to pay for stamp duty (see Fig. 8 on the next page).

FIG. 8 - COMBINATION STRATEGY METHOD

The Valuation Strategy For Buyers	This strategy is based on the Seller giving a Cash Incentive that is related to the VALUATION of the property, and will apply whenever prices of comparable properties are higher. Use this strategy when price reduction is nil or not sufficient *and* prices of COMPARABLES are higher (If price is the same or lower, use *The Price Strategy For Buyers*)
The Price Strategy For Buyers	This strategy is based on the Seller giving a Cash Incentive that is equivalent to the price reduction the Seller is willing to give, and will apply whenever *The Valuation Strategy For Buyers* cannot be used. Use this strategy when price reduction is nil or not sufficient *and* prices of COMPARABLES are the same or lower (If price is higher, use *The Valuation Strategy For Buyers*)

Fig. 8 shows when to use these strategies, so that *whatever the comparables* we still have a viable strategy for getting a big Cash Incentive and overcoming a property price that is too high.

Combining these two strategies is at the heart of stamp duty planning, and to thoroughly appreciate how this works several examples follow. Study these examples carefully as they show how the strategy works in practice.

Example 1.

1. Asking price for apartment is £150,000.

2. Price is negotiated down to £148,000.

3. Using *The Price Strategy For Buyers* you could ask the Seller to agree to a £2,000 Cash Incentive. But prior to negotiating the deal you checked the COMPARABLES and established that the best similar apartments nearby have sold at about £155,000.

4. Since the COMPARABLES are higher than the <u>asking price</u> of £150,000 you decide to use *The Valuation Strategy For Buyers*. So you go on to ask for a £7,000 Cash Incentive. Note that £7,000 is the total of the price reduction (£2,000) and the COMPARABLES (on average £5,000 higher).

5. If the COMPARABLES had been about the same or lower than the asking price, you would have used *The Price Strategy For Buyers* and just asked for a £2,000 Cash Incentive. However, in this scenario you would have added the cost of stamp duty to the asking price (say £1,500), giving you a Cash Incentive of £3,500.

6. Naturally, you would also use any of the other strategies that may apply.

Example 2.

1. Asking price for apartment is £150,000.

2. Price is negotiated down to £146,000.

3. Using *The Price Strategy For Buyers* you could ask the Seller to agree to a £4,000 Cash Incentive. But prior to negotiating the deal you checked the COMPARABLES and established that the best similar apartments nearby have sold at about £150,000.

4. Since the COMPARABLES are similar to the <u>asking price</u> of £150,000 you decide to use *The Price Strategy For Buyers*. So you consider asking for a £4,000 Cash Incentive. Note that no Cash Incentive for the COMPARABLES can be realized because they are similar in price to the property you are buying.

5. If the COMPARABLES had been higher than the asking price, you would have used *The Valuation Strategy For Buyers*.

6. Since you are using *The Price Strategy For Buyers* you decide to combine the discount amount with the stamp duty amount and ask for a Cash Incentive of £5,500 (total of £4,000 discount plus £1,500 stamp duty). If this is not clear you should re-read *The Price Strategy For Buyers.*

7. Naturally, you would also use any of the other strategies that may apply.

Example 3.

1. Asking price for apartment is £150,000.

2. The COMPARABLES are similar in price.

3. A tiny price reduction of £500 is negotiated, bringing the payment amount down to 149,500. You risk losing the property if you don't agree to go ahead.

4. However, the house has a conservatory, whereas the three COMPARABLES that have been short listed do not have conservatories. This is a 'unique feature' and it puts the value of the target property up by £3,000 in relation to the comparables (remember that you must point this out to the Valuer when you meet him).

5. Note that if the target property had, for example, a bigger garden than the COMPARABLES the same principles apply. *Anything* that increases the value of the target property (compared to the COMPARABLES) can be used to increase the valuation – the higher the valuation, the bigger the Cash Incentive.

6. Using *The Valuation Strategy For Buyers* you agree a selling PRICE of £153,000 with a Cash Incentive of £3,500, giving the Seller a net amount of £149,500. Note that the £3,500 Cash Incentive is the total of the price reduction (£500) and the price difference of £3,000 (COMPARABLES at £150,000 and the target property plus conservatory at £153,000).

7. In this example you have combined *The Price Strategy For Buyers* and *The Valuation Strategy For Buyers* to get a Cash Incentive of £3,500. But note that you would only ever present one of these strategies to the Seller (otherwise

everybody would get confused!). Also, note that as soon as you realized you could use the conservatory to get a higher valuation, you knew that you would only be presenting *The Valuation Strategy For Buyers* to the Seller.

8. Naturally, you would also use any of the other strategies that may apply.

Example 4.

1. Asking price for apartment is £150,000.

2. The COMPARABLES are similar in price.

3. A big price reduction of £5,000 is negotiated, as some renovation work is required, bringing the payment amount down to £145,000.

4. The house has a converted second toilet under the stairs, so you check the COMPARABLES and discover the following:

   a. COMPARABLE one has no second toilet and was sold for £149,000.

   b. COMPARABLE two has no second toilet and was sold for £148,000.

   c. COMPARABLE three has a second toilet and was sold for £152,000.

5. You decide to use all three COMPARABLES and you will tell the Valuer that as the property you are buying has a converted second toilet the value is about £152,000 (same as comparable number 3).

6. You know straight away that you will only be using *The Valuation Strategy For Buyers* with the Seller because you are going for a valuation that is greater than the asking price of the target property. So you will be agreeing a PRICE of £152,000 with a Cash Incentive of £7,000. Note that £7,000 is the total of the price reduction (£5,000) and the valuation price difference of £2,000 (the COMPARABLE with the second toilet is on average £2,000 higher than the asking price of £150,000).

7. In this example you have combined *The Price Strategy For Buyers* and *The Valuation Strategy For Buyers* to get a Cash Incentive of £7,000. But note that you would only ever present one of these strategies to the Seller (otherwise everybody gets confused!). Also, note that as soon as you realized you could use the converted toilet to get a higher valuation, you knew that you would only be presenting *The Valuation Strategy For Buyers* to the Seller, even though the price reduction was *greater* than the valuation difference.

8. Naturally, you would also use any of the other strategies that may apply.

Example 5.

1. A house is for sale at £230,000. The Buyer knows he is able to get a 95% mortgage but has little money for the 5% deposit. So he offers £221,000 as this would reduce the amount of deposit he would have to pay the Lender.

2. After negotiations, the Seller comes down to £226,000 and will not reduce the price any further. There is a real risk that the Buyer will lose the house as there is a price gap of £4,000.

3. To resolve the problem the Buyer decides to ask the Seller for a £9,000 Cash Incentive by combining *The Valuation Strategy For Buyers* and *The Price Strategy For Buyers*.

4. Let's recap the situation so far in this example: The asking price was £230,000 and the Buyer offered £221,000 but this was rejected. The best reduction offered by the Seller was £226,000 (a price reduction of £4,000). The buyer is keen to get the property but does not have enough money for the 5% deposit so he decides to ask the Seller for a £9,000 Cash Incentive. Fig. 9 on the next page summarizes the possible scenarios.

FIG. 9 - CASH INCENTIVE REQUEST

(Example 5)

	A (£) Adver- tised price	B (£) Buyer's offer	C (£) Seller's minimum price	D (£) Buyer's proposal
Selling price	230,000	221,000	226,000	235,000
Cash-incentive	Not applicabl e	Not applicable	Not applicable	9,000
Net amount received by seller	230,000	221,000 (cannot be accepted)	226,000	226,000
Buyer's loan based on 95% mortgage	218,500	209,950	214,700	223,250
Buyer's deposit based on 5%	11,500	11,050	11,300	11,750
Less Cash Incentive	none	none	none	9,000
Amount required for deposit	11,500	11,050	11,300	2,750

Column A is the original price advertised by the Seller. Column B is the best 'conventional' offer the Buyer can make in the hope of reducing the deposit. This offer cannot be accepted by the Seller, but even if it were accepted the deposit amount would only be reduced by £450!

Column C shows the best offer the Seller is willing to accept. This would leave the Buyer with a deposit of £11,300 instead of £11,500 (still too much). Column D shows the proposal made by the Buyer to secure the house and give the Seller a deal he will accept.

Reading from left to right in the bottom row you can see that the deposit amount does not vary significantly until you get to the

Cash Incentive deal which has a direct impact on the deposit. Clearly, if using a Cash Incentive to finance a mortgage deposit, a Buyer may have to obtain a bridging loan for two or three days (the time interval between paying the deposit to the solicitor to complete the deal and receiving the Cash Incentive to repay the bridging loan).

Most people are held back from buying a property because of the deposit required by the mortgage company. They try to resolve this by negotiating a lower price. But note that any reduction in price has an insignificant effect on the deposit.

The solution, in this example, is to combine *The Valuation Strategy For Buyers* with *The Discount Strategy For Buyers* and get a big Cash Incentive of £9,000. Only The *Valuation Strategy For Buyers* would be presented to the Seller. Naturally, the Buyer will have done his homework and established that getting a valuation of £235,000 is feasible.

The £9,000 Cash Incentive is the total of the £4,000 price reduction plus the £5,000 price increase. So the selling price is £235,000 and the mortgage is based on this figure. The money for the £9,000 Cash Incentive is money left over from the mortgage loan, given that the actual amount paid for the house is £226,000. To be clear: The mortgage company gives £235,000 to the Seller, but as the Seller has agreed to accept only £226,000, he returns £9,000 to the Buyer in the form of a Cash Incentive.

In this example the Seller is happy as he gets the minimum of £226,000 he wanted. The Buyer is happy as he did not lose the house and only had to pay £2,750 deposit instead of £11,750. Of course, against this the Buyer has a slightly bigger mortgage to pay off. But the extra interest is very small compared to the advantages of gaining a valuable property asset and paying a much smaller deposit.

This solution has given the Buyer a home and saved him much more than the cost of stamp duty. It has also enabled the Seller to get a successful sale, and the Lender to get a new client. Even the tax authorities are happy as they get paid stamp duty on a higher SELLING PRICE. Everybody wins!

Summary of *The Combination Strategy For Buyers*:

1. Study all the strategies for avoiding stamp duty and use those that best apply to your particular property deal.

2. Take advantage of Cash Incentives from the Seller, the Lender, and the Mortgage Broker, whenever possible. There is no reason why several Cash Incentives cannot be applied to the same property transaction.

3. Do your homework before negotiating with the Seller: check out the COMPARABLES as you need to know these for applying *The Price Strategy For Buyers* or *The Valuation Strategy For Buyers*.

4. Use low-priced COMPARABLES to help you negotiate a price reduction in the conventional manner. Use high-priced COMPARABLES to help you get a high valuation from the Valuer.

5. Get a *Cash Incentive* whether COMPARABLES are higher, lower, or similar to the property you are buying. Do this by using both *The Price Strategy For Buyers* and *The Valuation Strategy For Buyers* but only present one of these strategies to the Seller.

6. Get a *Cash Incentive* whether or not a lower price can be negotiated. Do this by using both *The Price Strategy For Buyers* and *The Valuation Strategy For Buyers* but only present one of these strategies to the Seller.

PART TWO

PROPERTY SELLERS

Introduction

When buying or selling property this book can save you thousands of pounds. When you *buy* a property you will save at least the cost of stamp duty, and when you *sell* you will be able to offer the property free of stamp duty to get a better response (and even a better price). Either way you will win every time.

This book focuses on the buying and selling of property in the UK. PARTS 1 and 2 cover residential property. PART 3 covers other ways of avoiding stamp duty, including land, commercial and non-residential property.

Most of the stamp-duty-avoidance strategies described in this book cannot be used in property auctions unless you can negotiate direct with the Seller, and have the property withdrawn from auction. Basically, the strategies in this book depend on some kind of direct contact between Buyer and Seller, or their estate agents.

Note that in Scotland, property transactions are often *negotiated* through solicitors. Therefore, if you are buying or selling property in Scotland you are urged to make *direct contact with the Buyer or Seller* as applicable. The fact that conveyancing laws in Scotland are different to the rest of the UK should not affect the principles and strategies covered in this book.

You may be wondering how it is possible to *legally* avoid paying stamp duty on property. Clearly, the tax authorities are not going to be deprived of their tax, so what we are talking about here is a mix of legal avoidance, paying *less*, and making *savings*. For example, you will see how a Buyer can pay nil stamp duty on properties up to £150,000, or pay £2,000 in stamp duty instead of, say, £5,000. Or how a Buyer can make a saving in the property transaction that is equal to or greater than the amount of stamp duty. The net result is that the Buyer can usually avoid most or all of the cost of stamp duty.

Using these strategies Sellers can benefit by being able to bridge a price gap. For example if an offer to buy falls short by £4,000, the Seller can use the strategies in this book to bridge the £4,000 gap and get the full asking price. Also, the book shows Sellers how to best offer a property for sale 'free of stamp duty' as a means of generating interest and getting a sale.

A major brake on selling a property is the amount of 'money down' that a *Buyer* has to come up with to buy a property. The 'money down' is the cash required *but not covered* by the mortgage, such as legal fees, stamp duty, and the mortgage deposit. If a Seller can offer a property for sale with 'no money down' it's a great way to get a sale, and this book shows how.

Several powerful stamp-duty-avoidance strategies are explained in this book; a kind of à-la-carte menu of stamp-duty-avoidance strategies. A brief summary is given at the end of each strategy – but please do not be tempted to just read the summaries as you will miss valuable tips and explanations.

In practice you will be using two or three of these strategies whenever selling property to give you a profitable and quick sale. Such strategies are special and effective, and at least one is likely to work each time you sell a property. If you trade in property professionally such strategies will help to ensure the success of your business.

This book is written as an instruction manual, and as such, it contains step-by-step procedures with easy to follow examples. Some points are repeated for added emphasis and to aid comprehension.

To fully appreciate the savings involved let's look at stamp duty costs. The rates of stamp duty are as shown in fig. 1:

FIG. 1 - RATES OF STAMP DUTY

Property Price	Stamp Duty
Not more than £120,000	0%
More than £120,000 but not more than £250,000	1%
More than £250,000 but not more than £500,000	3%
More than £500,000	4%

This means that on a house worth £200,000 a Buyer would pay £2,000 in stamp duty. And as soon as you get up to say £300,000, the stamp duty climbs to £9,000! So clearly stamp duty amounts to thousands of pounds, rather than hundreds, and the amounts are of major significance when considering just about any property transaction.

Stamp duty is short for *'Stamp Duty Land Tax'* and is often abbreviated to SDLT in official documents. In this book we will refer to it simply as 'stamp duty'. But what exactly is stamp duty? In the context of property or land, stamp duty is nothing more than a property tax. The tax is based on the purchase value of the property.

The tax authorities make no distinction between the property and the fixtures and fittings attached to the property. In other words, fixtures and fittings are also taxable. So if a house is bought for £100,000 and you reckon the fixtures and fittings are worth £3,000, you cannot pay stamp duty on only £97,000. This is discussed in more detail in the chapter *'The Threshold Strategy For Sellers'*.

When a Buyer pays stamp duty the solicitor passes the money onto the tax authorities together with the address of the property. This is done by using a special form that is signed by the Buyer.

A property Buyer will find that when he receives his solicitor's bill the stamp duty will be listed along with other disbursements such as valuation fees, legal fees, deposits, money transfer costs, and the like.

So the requirement to pay stamp duty cannot be avoided, but the powerful strategies about to be examined will enable a Seller to give the Buyer a Cash Incentive without the Seller suffering any financial loss. By doing so, the Seller is able to offer the property at a more competitive price, get a higher price, or bridge a price gap to clinch a deal.

For ease of reference, this publication falls into two parts: *Part One* for people who are BUYING a property. *Part Two* for those SELLING a property. Each part is completely self-contained, as if they were two separate books. Therefore, the reader's forbearance is appreciated where duplication appears.

You need to read both parts when buying *and* selling (which is often the case if you are moving house). Please do not be tempted to skip pages or you may miss important information – study each page carefully and it will repay you handsomely.

Some aspects of the strategies presented here may not apply to each and every property transaction. But certainly some aspects of the strategies *will* apply, particularly if you are buying or selling property and are able to deal directly with the Buyer or Seller (or with an estate agent). Therefore, as you read this book you are bound to discover 'golden nuggets' that best apply to your situation, and you will be able to start using them straight away to make your property sales more successful and profitable.

In this book the words 'he/his' are used to include 'she/hers.'

Financial Terms Used

Several financial terms referred to in this book come into play when buying or selling property:

1. **PRICE.** This is the purchase price agreed with the seller and is the figure entered on all the paperwork (including the Land Registry) as the SELLING PRICE. This is also the figure that will be used by the Lender or Mortgage Company to work out how much money to lend. Note that the PRICE does not include PURCHASE COSTS (see below).

2. **TRANSACTION COSTS.**

   - These are the additional costs incurred when buying or selling a property, and include legal fees, conveyancing fees, estate agent fees, surveyor costs, valuation costs, council searches, renovation costs, buildings insurance, stamp duty, payments for fixtures, fittings, carpets, furniture and the like.

   - Clearly some TRANSACTION COSTS may not apply to a particular property sale, but others will always apply the point being that the Buyer's COSTS cannot normally be included in the loan or mortgage. The Buyer has to find the money for his TRANSACTION COSTS from personal savings or other sources. This aspect is at the heart of stamp-duty-avoidance strategies used by a Buyer or Seller.

3. **LOAN.** This is the amount of money borrowed to buy a property (referred to as the mortgage or loan). The amount of the LOAN is based on the PRICE. For example, a 95% LTV (Loan To Value) means that you get a loan that is equivalent to 95% of the PRICE. The expression *Loan To Value* is used (rather than Loan To Price) because Lenders base the amount of the loan on the <u>valuation</u> that they carry out before giving you the money. Provided that the valuation is not *lower* than the PRICE, you will get a loan based on the PRICE. In the United Kingdom you can typically get LOANS that vary between 70% and 100% of the PRICE. If the LOAN is 100% you will borrow an amount of money equal to the PRICE, and hence not have to pay a deposit.

4. **DEPOSIT.** This is the amount paid towards the PRICE. For example, if a Buyer gets a 95% LOAN, the deposit is the

balance of 5%. Where funds are scarce a person will naturally opt for as big a LOAN as possible, thus minimizing the DEPOSIT.

5. **CONVEYANCING COSTS.** These relate to the legal fees, valuation fees, council searches, stamp duty, and other costs applied by solicitors or conveyancers on both sides. Normally, the amount of the LOAN taken out by a Buyer does not take into account any CONVEYANCING COSTS; in other words, a Buyer cannot ask the Lender to provide extra money for CONVEYANCING COSTS. The terms LEGAL COSTS and CONVEYANCING COSTS are interchangeable in this book.

Clearly there is an overlap between the TRANSACTION COSTS and the CONVEYANCING COSTS in the sense that many of the same costs come under both headings. The point to keep in mind is that some TRANSACTION COSTS are not channelled through the solicitor, e.g. the Seller may agree to sell some furniture to the Buyer without involving their respective Solicitors.

The stamp duty is shown under two headings: TRANSACTION COSTS *and* CONVEYANCING COSTS. Typically, *the Buyer* will pay the stamp duty to the solicitor (this is not normally included in the LOAN), and the solicitor will pay it on to the Inland Revenue with details of the address. There is no legal way to avoid the payment of stamp duty when a property transaction requires that stamp duty be applied. However, this book shows how this cost can be recovered (or reduced), so that in effect you end up not incurring the cost of stamp duty.

The six stamp-duty-avoidance-strategies that follow are shown in Fig.2 (on the next page).

FIG. 2 - SIX STAMP DUTY AVOIDANCE STRATEGIES FOR SELLERS

1	The Tax Exemption Strategy For Sellers
2	The Threshold Strategy For Sellers
3	The Link Strategy For Sellers
4	The Price Strategy For Sellers
5	The Valuation Strategy For Sellers
6	The Combination Strategy For Sellers

Stamp Duty Avoidance Strategy No. 1:

The Tax Exemption Strategy For Sellers

In the UK there are literally hundreds of 'Designated Disadvantaged Areas' (DDAs) spread all over the country, although there are not many in the more affluent shires of South East England. Glasgow for example has many DDAs. The point is this: If a residential property is sold in a DDA no stamp duty will be payable by the Buyer if the value is not over £150,000. If the value is over £150,000 the normal rules apply.

Note: Stamp duty rules for commercial property (i.e. non-residential property) are the same, whether located in a DDA or not. In other words, there is no stamp duty relief for commercial property by virtue of being located in a DDA.

So if you are selling a residential property, it is worth checking whether the property is in a DDA. If it is not, this particular strategy cannot be applied. If the property *is* in a DDA, it means you have more flexibility to offer the property for sale 'free of stamp duty'.

DDAs are also referred to as *Enterprise Areas* because the government wants to encourage economic growth in such areas (hence the stamp duty concession).

To see a list of DDAs on the Internet (too many to list here) go to **http://www.inlandrevenue.gov.uk/so/disadvantaged.htm**.
Alternatively, go to
http://www.inlandrevenue.gov.uk/so/pcode_search.htm which allows postcodes to be entered to check if within a DDA.

You can also enquire about DDAs or *Enterprise Areas* by phoning the Stamp Taxes Helpline on 0845 603 0135. Clearly, poor or neglected areas are more likely to be in a DDA than millionaires' row!

A property can be offered for sale 'free of stamp duty' even if stamp duty applies. It simply means that the *Seller* would incur the cost of the stamp duty, which can in some circumstances be advantageous (more on this in the chapter covering *The Threshold Strategy For Sellers*). The actual mechanics for a Seller to pay stamp duty are simple: give the money to the Buyer, either in cash or by adjusting the selling price. Note that the stamp duty payment form must be signed by the Buyer as it is a personal declaration of tax.

When selling a property in a DDA it is important for both the Buyer and Seller to tell their respective solicitors that a stamp duty exemption applies (this is not automatically checked by the tax authorities and many solicitors are not very aware of DDAs).

Summary of *The Tax Exemption Strategy For Sellers*:

1. In the UK there are many DDAs (Designated Disadvantaged Areas). Any property bought in a DDA is exempt from stamp duty if the value is not over £150,000.

2. DDAs tend to be more common in poor or neglected areas, in both rural and urban communities. To check if a property might be located in a DDA go to **http://www.inlandrevenue.gov.uk/so/disadvantaged.htm** or telephone 0845 603 0135.

3. If selling a property in a DDA (also known as an *Enterprise Area*) you can benefit be being able to offer the property for sale 'free of stamp duty'. This helps to attract buyers or make the price more competitive compared to similar properties in non-DDA areas.

4. If taking advantage of a DDA as a Seller, be sure to tell your solicitor to tell the Buyer's solicitor that no stamp duty will apply.

The Threshold Strategy For Sellers

This strategy is about helping the Buyer pay less stamp duty on the property you are selling to your mutual benefit. More specifically, this strategy helps the Buyer legally avoid paying a higher rate of stamp duty than necessary. For properties priced close to the first threshold of £120,000 it may be possible to avoid stamp duty altogether.

As mentioned, the rates of stamp duty are as follows:

Property Price	Stamp Duty
Not more than £120,000	0%
More than £120,000 but not more than £250,000	1%
More than £250,000 but not more than £500,000	3%
More than £500,000	4%

In this strategy we will be concerned with three tax thresholds:

- Paying nil duty instead of 1% duty.
- Paying 1% duty instead of 3% duty.
- Paying 3% duty instead of 4% duty.

For instance, a property priced at £250,000 incurs stamp duty at 1% (£2,500). But a property priced at £250,001 incurs stamp duty at 3% (£7,500.03). So just by moving down to a lower threshold by making a small change in the price, the potential savings can amount to thousands of pounds.

It therefore does not make sense to sell a property priced just over the threshold of £250,000 as this is likely to create Buyer resistance. In fact you will rarely find properties priced in the £251,000 - £260,000 bracket precisely for this reason. A similar analogy applies to the £500,000 threshold.

In practice, Estate Agents and Sellers tend to avoid offering prices in the £250-£260k bracket, but you sometimes see prices at £259,000 or £260,000. The first £15,000 after the threshold tends to be 'forbidden territory'. In other words there are few properties priced between £250,000 and £265,000. This can be verified by looking in any property newspaper and in estate agents' windows.

We can take advantage of this. Fig.3 shows how.

FIG. 3 - THE THRESHOLDS

OMV = Open Market Value
THRESHOLDS = £120,000 or £250,000 or £500,000, whichever most applies to your property deal.

Item	Seller's Perceived OMV (£)	Seller's asking price (£)	Potential price reduction (£)
1	Under the threshold	Under the threshold	May or may not be negotiable
2	Less than 2% over the threshold	The threshold price	Not very negotiable
3	Between 2% and 4% over the threshold	Between 2% and 4% over the threshold	Very negotiable
4	Between 4% and 10% over the threshold	Between 4% and 10% over the threshold	Not very negotiable
5	More than 10% over the threshold	More than 10% over the threshold	The threshold strategy becomes irrelevant

Item 1 in Fig. 3 shows that if the Seller/agent thinks the OMV (Open Market Value) is, for example, under £250,000, the stamp duty threshold of £250,000 is irrelevant and the price may or may not be negotiable.

Item 2 Fig. 3 shows that if the Seller/agent thinks the OMV is, for example, £253,000, a price reduction is unlikely to be granted as the price has already been reduced to £250,000 to bring it below the stamp duty threshold.

Item 3 in Fig 3 show that if the Seller/agent thinks the OMV is, for example, £257,000, and the asking price is £257,000, there is a good chance of negotiating the price down to £250,000 because the Seller/agent knows this will save the Buyer significant stamp duty. In another example, if the Seller/agent thinks the OMV is £125,000, and the asking price is £125,000, there is a good chance of negotiating the price down to £120,000 and avoiding stamp duty altogether.

Item 4 in Fig. 3 shows that if the Seller/agent thinks the OMV is, for example, £267,500 a price reduction to £250,000 is unlikely to be granted because it would be too big a reduction. The Seller/agent has decided to not take the stamp duty threshold into account in setting a selling price as it would be too much of a 'sacrifice'. However, there is still the possibility of negotiating a discount, but not enough to reach the lower threshold.

Item 5 in Fig 3 shows that if the Seller/agent thinks the OMV is, for example, £280,000, a price reduction to £250,000 is likely to be out of the question, and therefore the threshold strategy cannot be used.

The strategy for the Seller then is to avoid the item 3 scenario in Fig. 3 above. That is, avoid offering a property for sale that is priced close to but over the threshold, *unless you are willing to come down in price*.

For example, don't offer a property for sale at £125,000 unless you are willing to reduce the price to £120,000. If you offer the property for sale at £125,000 you will create Buyer resistance in just about every case, as Buyers will want to bring the price down to £120,000 in order to avoid paying 1% stamp duty. It is better to sell at £120,000, or if you think it is worth more, then £135,000.

Here is an example of how the negotiation might go. Let's assume you think your house is worth at least £260,000, but you are keen to sell. You therefore offer the house at £259,000. As this is £9,000 above the tax threshold, you know you are bound to be asked to reduce the price to £250,000, but for you this is too little. In the example that follows we will assume you are willing to accept £255,000 as your rock bottom price.

EXAMPLE

Buyer: *'You are selling the house for £259,000 is that correct?'*

Seller: *'Yes, the price is £259,000 and includes all the fixtures and fittings already discussed.'*

Buyer: *Would you be willing to reduce the price to £250,000 as this would save me a lot of money in stamp duty.*

Seller: *Yes, I understand that you would save stamp duty by only paying 1% instead of 3%, so I have a special proposition. May I explain it to you?*

Buyer: *Okay, what do you have in mind?*

Seller: *Well, if you were to buy the house for £259,000 you would have to pay £7,770 in stamp duty. If your buy the house at £250,000 the stamp duty is only £2,500, so I want to suggest a compromise. I am willing to sell the house at £250,000 so that you can save stamp duty costs. But additionally, I want you to agree to buy a list of chattels from me amounting to £5,000.*

Buyer: *This sounds interesting. So what is the total amount I would pay? Would it be £250,000 plus £2,500 stamp duty, plus £5,000 for chattels?*

Seller: *Yes, the total would be £257,500. Let me go through the list of chattels with you so that you can decide what to do.*

(Later)

Buyer: *If I agree to this, how would the money for the chattels be handed over?*

Seller: *'My solicitor will confirm to your solicitor that I have agreed to sell a list of chattels, and the additional £5,000 would be paid by your solicitor upon completion. Do we have a deal? If so, I will confirm in writing the list of chattels so that we all know what is being left behind at the property.*

Buyer: *'That sounds good. We may have a deal. Let's finalize the list of chattels.'*

Here are some tips for preparing the list of chattels:

- Take care that any amounts allocated to 'Chattels', such as carpets and curtains, are properly supportable. So in this example, the items listed need to reflect a realistic value of £5,000 *in the eyes of the tax authorities*. Of course, you the Seller may not regard the chattels as being worth £5,000 (you may think they are worth much more or much less, but that is not so relevant).

- Fixtures and fittings are not allowed as they are taxable. Therefore, only chattels (things that can be moved) are allowable.

- The List must be genuine, and the goods on the list must exist. This must be so even though the transaction may be viewed as a vehicle for paying money to the Seller (in this example £5,000). The Seller should not try to 'get his money's worth'. Rather, he should try to find the right balance between a worthless list and a supportable list.

- As many items as possible should be included on the list, however inconsequential and small the value. For example, include, if possible, all kitchen appliances and equipment. The longer the list the better.

- Do not enter money values for each item. Only enter the total value (e.g. £5,000).

- Do not enter terms such as 'fixtures and fittings' or 'floor coverings' or 'kitchen appliances' or 'Chattels'. Avoid generic names. Enter an individual name/description for each item.

Warning

The UK tax authorities do not like property transactions that include a large payment for 'chattels' (also known as 'movables') as a way of avoiding stamp duty. In particular they are likely to challenge and investigate a payment for chattels if the amount exceeds 10% of the price of the property. To play safe, any payment for chattels should not exceed 5% of the price of the property. Furthermore, the items sold as chattels must be worth the amount paid. Therefore, the more substantive the list of items the better.

In the above example the buyer would pay £257,500 for the house (£250,000 plus 1% stamp duty, plus £5,000). This compares against £266,770 without a reduction (£259,000 plus 3% stamp duty). So, as a result of using this strategy, the Seller has made a sale and saved the Buyer £9,270!

Of course, you ended up getting £255,000 instead of the £259,000 asking price, but that's better than £250,000, and you can move on with your life.

Is it legal to offer to sell chattels in this way? Yes it is provided the chattels are genuine. This is what the tax authorities have to say on the matter (the following is a summarized extract from the Inland Revenue):

> 'For an item to be regarded as a fixture as opposed to a chattel (called 'moveable' in Scotland), the item must be fixed to the property. Where a purchaser agrees to buy a property for a price that includes an amount properly attributed to chattels, that amount will not be charged to Stamp Duty.
>
> In recent times an increasing number of cases have arisen in which the amount of money attributed to chattels is more than a small percentage of the total amount. This has been particularly noticeable where the chargeable amount is brought just below the £250,000 or £500,000 stamp duty thresholds.
>
> Under the Stamp Duty regime a "just and reasonable apportionment" is required where a price is paid partly for a property and partly for chattels. It does not matter that the parties to a transaction may agree a particular apportionment, which is then documented in the contract. The apportionment will not be correct unless it was arrived at on a "just and reasonable" basis.
>
> The Inland Revenue has the right to make enquiries into the property transaction and into cases where a deduction has been made for chattels, to confirm that those items properly fall within the definition of chattels. The Inland Revenue is unable to provide a comprehensive list of items that it accepts as chattels because each case must be considered on its own merits and because this is an area of the law that continues to evolve.

The following are, however, confirmed as being items that will normally be regarded as chattels:

- *Carpets (fitted or otherwise).*
- *Curtains and Blinds.*
- *Free standing furniture.*
- *Kitchen white goods.*
- *Electric and Gas fires (provided that they can be removed by disconnection from the power supply without causing damage to the property).*
- *Light shades and fittings (unless recessed).*
- *Plants and shrubs growing in pots or containers (internally or externally).*

On the other hand, the following will <u>not</u> normally be regarded as chattels:

- *Fitted kitchen units, cupboards and sinks.*
- *Gas ovens and wall mounted ovens.*
- *Fitted bathroom sanitary ware.*
- *Central heating systems.*
- *Intruder alarm systems.*
- *Plants, shrubs or trees growing in the soil.*

It is clear, then, that the tax authorities will allow a separate payment from Buyer to Seller for 'Chattels' provided that any stamp-duty-avoidance is incidental to the transaction rather than the sole purpose. It is also clear that such chattels may include fitted carpets, white kitchen goods, fitted curtains, removable gas and electric fires, and many items which traditionally have been thought of as 'fixtures and fittings'.

In fact the term 'fixtures and fittings' should not come into the transaction as matters can get confused. It is best to only think in terms of chattels (or 'movables' in Scotland).

There is a misconception that the value of 'fixtures and fittings' must be accounted for and added to the price of the property for stamp duty purposes. This is not so. The tax authorities regard fixtures and fittings as a taxable part of the property. If fixtures and fittings are charged for separately this cost must be added to the selling price, and stamp duty will be payable on the grand total. Therefore, the tax authorities do not care whether fixtures and fittings are included in the price or charged for separately since it makes no difference to the amount of tax paid.

In practice, fixtures and fittings will normally be included in the SELLING PRICE and therefore do not need to be 'evaluated'. However, the fixtures and fittings do need to be listed and agreed so that there can be no misunderstanding over what the Seller is or is not leaving behind. This is standard practice, and solicitors use a ready made check list when agreeing fixtures and fittings.

The point about *The Threshold Strategy For Sellers* is that fixtures and fittings cannot be used as a means of receiving money from the Buyer, *but chattels can.* This is what it boils down to:

- A Buyer gets taxed on non-chattels (i.e. fixtures) and they *cannot be* used to negotiate a below-threshold price.

- A Buyer does not get taxed on chattels and they *can be* used to negotiate a below-threshold price (but to be safe don't make chattels more than 5% of the SELLING PRICE).

- Make sure that as many items as possible are listed as chattels rather than as 'fixtures and fittings'. That way the chattels list will be more substantial and acceptable to the tax authorities.

Summary of *The Threshold Strategy For Sellers*:

1. Properties should not be priced at *just over* the stamp duty thresholds of £120,000, £250,000, and £500,000 **unless you are willing to negotiate** as this creates buyer resistance.
2. To overcome Buyer resistance without losing out (and to attract interest) the Seller can offer a property that is higher than the threshold, and then be willing to negotiate a lower price, which may or may not include selling chattels.
3. If there is any possibility of selling chattels, prepare the list in advance. This is a list of movable things that can be offered to a Buyer in return for a sum of money. The longer the list the better. Make sure that no possible chattels get included on the 'fixtures and fittings' list prepared by the solicitor. Use the chattels list in your negotiations. Think of the chattels list as a vehicle for receiving money from the Buyer.

The Link Strategy For Sellers

This strategy will reduce the amount of stamp duty from 4% to 3%, or from 3% to 1% (or even 4% to 1%), giving a huge potential saving. It will only suit a property Seller who may want to sell more than one property to the same Buyer, either as a lot, or as a series of transactions over time. It will also suit anybody selling at auction.

Property developers and Sellers can benefit from this strategy as follows:

1. Sell more than one property to the *same* Buyer without attracting a higher rate of stamp duty.

2. Build repeat business and customer loyalty with property investors without making Buyers pay stamp duty at a higher rate.

3. Offer property free of stamp duty without financial loss as a way of generating greater buyer interest and achieving greater success.

The Link Strategy For Sellers is for a Seller who wants to help a Buyer avoid falling into a **stamp duty tax trap,** a trap that most people have never heard of. By helping a Buyer in this way, the Seller benefits in the three ways mentioned above. People get caught in the **stamp duty tax trap** just about every week of the year, forcing them to pay much more stamp duty than necessary.

The Tax Trap

If selling two or more properties to the same person or company there is a likelihood that the transaction will be regarded as 'linked' for stamp duty tax purposes. This is so even if there is a time gap between selling each property. For example, if selling two properties each priced at £150,000, the stamp duty rate would be 3% for each property rather than 1% (because, in this example, the total of £300,000 is above the stamp duty threshold of £250,000). In this example, the *extra* stamp duty the Buyer pays is £6,000. By using **The Link Strategy For Sellers,** you can potentially help a Buyer make savings of tens of thousands of pounds, depending on the prices of the properties.

It is appreciated that the Buyer pays the stamp duty and not the Seller. But if the seller can package the offer so as to avoid linkage, the savings in stamp duty can 'shared' between Buyer and Seller in a variety of ways.

When the linked rule comes into play the extra stamp duty paid can be very substantial. If you want to get repeat business from professional property investors, it is important to be aware of *linked transactions* (the tax trap).

Section 108 of *The Finance Act 2003* has a section titled 'Linked Transactions' which reads as follows:

> ### 108 Linked transactions
>
> *(1) Transactions are 'linked' for the purposes of this Part if they form part of a single scheme, arrangement or series of transactions between the same vendor and purchaser or, in either case, persons connected with them.*
>
> *Section 839 of the Taxes Act 1988 (connected persons) has effect for the purposes of this subsection*
>
> *(2) Where there are two or more linked transactions with the same effective date, the purchaser, or all of the purchasers if there is more than one, may make a single land transaction return as if all of those transactions that are notifiable were a single notifiable transaction.*
>
> *(3) Where two or more purchasers make a single return in respect of linked transactions, section 103 (joint purchasers) applies as if-*
> *(a) the transactions in question were a single transaction, and*
> *(b) those purchasers were purchasers acting jointly.*

What this means is that if you are selling more than one property to the same Buyer, then according to *The Finance Act 2003*, the transaction is linked and the Buyer has to pay stamp duty **at a rate** based on the *total value* of all the properties being purchased.

However, there are circumstances when there is no linkage even though you may be selling more than one property to the same person or company. And when there is no linkage the Buyer does not get clobbered with extra stamp duty! What are these circumstances? Here are some examples:

Example 1.

A house builder is selling flats. He makes a special offer: *'Buy two flats and you get a discount of 15% on the second flat.'* Peter bought the two flats and *benefited* from the discount. This kind of transaction is linked because they are both part of the same business deal. The stamp duty rate is therefore based on the total value of both flats (resulting in a big jump in stamp duty!).

Alternative scenario.

A house builder is selling flats. He makes a special offer: 5% discount plus stamp duty paid. Peter buys one flat on these terms. Then a week later (or a month later, or a year later) Peter sees an advertisement from the builder offering further flats for sale, based on the same terms: 5% discount plus stamp duty paid. Peter responds to the advertisement in writing, making reference to the advertisement, and making no reference to any other property deals. In this alternative scenario there is no link because there was *no awareness* of further flats being available until Peter saw the advertisement. When it came to buying the second property, the Buyer *did not benefit* from his association with the first property deal or with the Seller because he got no special terms based on a second purchase. In this alternative scenario the two key phrases are *no awareness* and *no benefit.* When there is *no awareness* and *no benefit,* there is no link.

Example 2.

A house builder is selling flats. He sells a flat to Peter at £150,000. Peter is so pleased with the deal that he goes back to the Builder a month later and buys a second flat. This kind of transaction is linked because they are both part of the same business deal, or series of business deals. Peter's decision to buy a second flat is

114

linked to his awareness of the first flat. The time gap of a month is immaterial – what counts here is the fact that the Buyer had knowledge that linked both transactions. When Peter bought the second flat he *benefited* from his knowledge of the first flat and from his association with the Seller. The stamp duty rate is therefore based on the total value of both flats. This means a portion of the stamp duty payable is 'backdated' to the first property.

Alternative scenario.

Let's suppose that the house builder sells a flat to Peter at £150,000. Peter is so pleased with the flat that he asks a friend to act as a scout and find him another flat in a similar price range. Peter has complete confidence in his friend and gives him full discretion to put down a reservation fee if he finds the right property. His friend does indeed find a great property and pays the reservation fee of £500. Peter is happy with this second deal but discovers a week later that the Seller is by coincidence the same person that sold him the first flat. In this alternative scenario there is no link because there was *no awareness* of the common ownership. Furthermore, Peter can provide documentary evidence showing that he instructed his friend to act for him. When it came to buying the second property, the Buyer *did not benefit* from his acquaintance with the owner of the first property. In this alternative scenario the two key phrases are *no awareness* and *no benefit*. When there is *no awareness* and *no benefit*, there is no link.

Example 3.

John is a developer and he sells a house to Peter. About a year later, John contacts Peter and tells him he has another good property to offer him; this time it's a flat. Peter buys the flat and rents it out. This kind of transaction is linked because they are both part of a series of business deals. The one-year time gap is immaterial. The stamp duty rate is therefore based on the total value of the house and the flat. This means a higher rate of stamp duty, and a portion of the stamp duty payable is 'backdated' to the first property.

Alternative scenario.

John is a developer and he sells a house to Peter. About a year later Peter decides he would like to buy a flat to rent out. He places an advertisement in the *property wanted* section of a suitable newspaper. John happens to see the advertisement and replies to it in writing, making reference to the advertisement. A deal is negotiated and Peter buys the flat without any reference to the house that he also purchased from John a year ago. In this alternative scenario there is no link because there was *no awareness* of the common ownership until John replied to the advertisement. Furthermore, Peter can provide documentary evidence showing that he advertised for a property and that John responded to the advertisement *in writing*. When it came to buying the second property, the Buyer *did not benefit* from his acquaintance with the owner of the first property. In this alternative scenario the two key phrases are *no awareness* and *no benefit*. When there is *no awareness* and *no benefit*, there is no link.

Example 4.

Peter buys a bungalow from John's building firm. A year later Peter sees an advertisement from John's firm offering a flat for sale. Peter responds to the advertisement 'without remembering' that a year earlier he had dealt with the same firm for the purchase of his bungalow. Peter has not benefited from any discounts or special offers even though he is buying from John for the second time. In fact, Peter got exactly the same terms as if he was buying from John for the first time (absolutely no special terms whatsoever).

This kind of transaction is linked because they are both part of a series of business deals. The one-year time gap is immaterial. The stamp duty rate is therefore based on the total value of the bungalow and the flat. This means a portion of the stamp duty payable is 'backdated' to the first bungalow. Peter cannot argue that he did not benefit from, and was not aware of, the common ownership. The fact is that the two deals are linked by virtue of having the same Seller, and Peter cannot prove otherwise. Without documentary proof you have no case because a 'linked transaction' is assumed unless you can prove otherwise.

Alternative scenario.

Peter buys a bungalow from John's building firm. A year later Peter goes to a property auction and buys a flat from John. Later Peter discovers that the flat bought at auction was owned by the same John that sold him a bungalow a year ago. Clearly, Peter was not aware that John was the owner at the time of bidding for the property, and clearly Peter never suggested to John that he should sell the flat at auction. In this alternative scenario there is no link because there was *no awareness* of the common ownership. When it came to buying the second property at auction, the Buyer *did not benefit* from his association with the first property or with the Seller. In this alternative scenario the two key phrases are *no awareness* and *no benefit*. When there is *no awareness* and *no benefit*, there is no link.

Example 5.

Peter is interested in buying two run-down flats in a city centre building. He checks them out through the estate agent and is informed *in writing* that they are both owned by *City Banking Corporation*, as a result of repossession. Peter goes to the property auction and successfully bids for the first flat. He decides he will try his luck and go for the second flat, and again he wins the bid. This kind of transaction is linked because they are both part of a succession of business deals. In any investigation by the tax authorities they will quickly discover that the estate agent informed Peter about the common ownership of the two flats. The stamp duty rate is therefore based on the total value of both flats (resulting in a big jump in stamp duty!).

Alternative scenario.

Peter is interested in buying two run-down flats in a city centre building. He checks them out through the estate agent but is not told who the owner is or that they both belong to the same owner. There is nothing in the paperwork or the Auction House brochure to indicate that both flats have a common owner. Peter buys both properties at auction. Later he discovers that both properties were owned by the *City Banking Corporation*. In this alternative scenario there is no link because there was *no awareness* of the common ownership. When it came to buying the second property at auction, the Buyer *did not benefit* from knowing he had just bought the first flat.   In this alternative scenario the two key phrases are *no awareness* and *no benefit*.   When there is *no awareness* and *no benefit*, there is no link.

Example 6.

John wants to sell two flats to Peter.   For buying two flats John offers Peter a special 5% discount on each flat. This is a linked transaction so stamp duty is paid at 3% instead of 1%.   However, by getting 5% discount Peter is better off even though he has to pay the additional stamp duty.   Peter therefore goes ahead with the deal on the basis of it being a linked transaction.

Alternative scenario.

John wants to sell two flats to Peter.   However, John offers to sell just one flat to Peter at a generous discount of 10%.   A week later Peter sees an advertisement from John and as a result of *seeing the advertisement* Peter decides to buy another flat. He tells his solicitor in writing that as a result of seeing the advertisement he wants to buy a property from John (throughout the proceedings Peter and John make no reference to any other property deals).   So Peter goes ahead and buys the second flat *without any discount.* Each transaction has been 'negotiated' separately with nothing to link them. Peter did *not use his awareness* of the first transaction to derive a benefit from the second transaction: as no discount was given *no benefit* was obtained.   Furthermore, at the time of buying the first property, Peter *did not contemplate* buying a second property.   As this is not a linked transaction, stamp duty is only paid at the rate of 1% (rather than 3%) for each property. The net result is that Peter bought two properties, paid stamp duty at 1%, and obtained a 10% discount on one of them.

Example 7.

This example shows how a Seller can use *The Link Strategy For Sellers* to offer two or more properties to the same Buyer, free of stamp duty and with no financial loss.

118

Scenario A (not using the strategy):

John owns several flats which he wants to sell to property professionals. The price of each flat is £160,000. John decides to offer a package deal: Buy two flats and pay just £150,000 per flat. As this is a linked transaction the Buyer pays £300,000, plus stamp duty at 3% = £9,000 stamp duty. The Seller receives £300,000.

The total costs for Buyer and Seller are as follows:

Table A

Total costs incurred by Buyer	Total money received by Seller
Two flats at £150,000 each = £300,000	Two flats at £150,000 each = £300,000
Plus stamp duty @ 3% = £9,000	(Stamp duty of £9,000 paid by Buyer)
TOTAL: £309,000	TOTAL: £300,000

Scenario B (using the strategy):

John owns several flats which he wants to sell to property professionals. The price of each flat is £160,000. John decides to offer each flat at £160,000 free of stamp duty plus a £5,000 Cash Incentive. John is very careful to emphasize there are no special discounts or other benefits for deals of two or more flats. Moreover, John does everything possible keep separate each property sale (separate paperwork, separate purchase date) so that there is no link between each property sale. This helps ensure that the stamp duty rate will only be 1% as there is no linkage. This is completely legal and ethical since he is not giving a benefit to anybody for buying two or more properties.

John explains that he cannot sell a property free of stamp duty, but he will give the Buyer the money to pay for the stamp duty, so the net result will be the same.

The total costs for Buyer and Seller are as follows: (see next page)

Table B

Total costs incurred by Buyer	Total money received by Seller
Two flats at £160,000 each = £320,000	Two flats at £160,000 each = £320,000
(Stamp duty of £3,200 is paid by Seller)	Less stamp duty @ 1% = £3,200
Less £12,000 Cash Incentive = £12,000	Less £12,000 Cash Incentive = £12,000
TOTAL: £308,000	TOTAL: £304,800

Note: The Cash Incentive would be paid by the Seller to the Buyer from the proceeds of sale. This would be done on completion of sale by the Seller's solicitor. If buying with a mortgage, the Buyer would declare the Cash Incentive on the mortgage application form. Lenders do not mind this, provided the valuation carried out by the Lender is in agreement with the selling price.

In comparing above tables A and B you can see that the Seller has been able to offer properties free of stamp duty with no financial loss. In fact, in this example, the Seller has made a gain of £4,800 by offering the property free of stamp duty! The beauty of this strategy is twofold:

(i)   The Seller can give the Buyer both options. In his advertising, he can offer the flats at £150,000 for buying two or more (with **stamp duty paid** and **Cash Incentive** options). Then, when explaining the options in detail, the Seller would go through the above two '*completely hypothetical*' scenarios.

(ii)   The Seller does not need to offer packages of two or more properties. Much better to sell the properties individually, each free of stamp duty and with a Cash Incentive. That way, buyers have more flexibility to come back again and buy another property on the same good terms. However, the Seller must be very careful to not offer any kind of benefit for repeat business, and he must fully co-operate with the Buyer so as not to create *linkage*.

Note that in Scenario B (using the strategy) the Buyer comes out better even though paying £160,000 instead of £150,000 per flat! What's happening here is that the savings in stamp duty (£3,200

instead of £9,000) are, in effect, being shared by the Buyer and the Seller, so both parties come out winning. The amount 'shared' by each party can be changed by simply changing the selling price or the Cash Incentive.

Perhaps the biggest advantage for the Seller (by using the strategy) is the ability to sell any number of flats to the same Buyer without letting the Buyer fall into the *Linked Transaction* trap. In this example, if selling just four flats to the same Buyer, the amount of stamp duty savings (that could be 'shared' between both parties) would amount to £19,200!

Example 8.

John sells a flat in a high rise building at £190,000, plus a parking bay in the basement at £18,000. This is regarded as a linked transaction because both properties are being sold to the same Buyer as part of a single arrangement or series of transactions. It does not matter whether the parking bay is a specific allocated bay or whether you are just selling the right to use any space in the car park. The stamp duty payable by the Buyer is therefore 1% of £208,000.

Alternative Scenario.

John sells a flat in a high rise building at £190,000 and the Buyer pays stamp duty at 1%. A month (or a year) later John contacts the same Buyer offers him a parking bay that has become available. This is not a linked transaction, because at the time of selling the flat the Buyer was not contemplating buying a parking bay and he was not aware that a parking bay was available. Furthermore, there is no documentary evidence to prove otherwise. The Buyer decides to accept the offer, and he buys the parking bay for £18,000. As this is not a linked transaction, the Buyer pays no stamp duty on the £18,000 because the amount is below the tax threshold of £120,000.

Note that if you are selling more than one property at auction to the *same* Buyer, the Buyer has to be careful about how to proceed. This is because the Buyer will want to have documentary evidence (should he be queried by the tax authorities) that he did **not benefit from** and had **no awareness of** the common ownership. The Seller must therefore take care to not create a paper trail that could prove the Buyer knew who the Seller was before buying the properties at auction. This should not be a problem because it is not usual to divulge Seller details in auction catalogues.

Another point is that a husband and wife are regarded as linked. A husband cannot sell one property to a Buyer, with his wife selling another, as a way of avoiding a linked transaction. The linkage between spouses also extends to immediate family. When it comes to other relatives or work colleagues, the law is vague in terms of what constitutes a 'connected person' so be wary.

To police matters relating to linked transactions, the Inland Revenue has set up a special department that is informally known as 'COP 10' (coppers come to mind!). COP 10 refers to the Inland Revenue *Code Of Practice* number 10 (a kind of charter). You can see the text of this charter on the Internet by going to **http://www.inlandrevenue.gov.uk/pdfs/cop10.htm**. Should the tax authorities suspect possible linkage the matter would typically be referred to COP 10 for investigation. The COP 10 code of practice explains how they investigate linked transactions and what documents and information would be required from the Buyer in the event of a query. These documents are:

- your name and tax reference number;
- full particulars of the transaction or event in question;
- copies of all relevant documents with the relevant parts or passages identified;
- your opinion of the tax consequences of the particular transaction;
- your explanation of the particular point(s) of difficulty that led to your request;
- details of what sections of the Taxes Acts you consider to be relevant;

- particulars of any case law, Inland Revenue extra-statutory concessions or Statements of Practice you consider to be relevant;

- your reasons for your opinion of the tax consequences of the transaction.

Typically, COP 10 can rule on whether a particular property transaction is to be regarded as linked or not linked for stamp duty purposes. Naturally, if a Seller or Buyer were to discuss a particular scenario *before* the event, it must be entirely hypothetical. A Buyer can hardly claim at a later date that he had no **awareness** if he previously discussed the deal with COP 10, so tread with caution! COP 10 can be contacted as follows (this address acts for the whole of the UK):

COP 10
Manchester Stamp Office
Upper Fifth Floor
Royal Exchange
Exchange Street
Manchester, M2 7EV

Tel: 0161 834 8109

It is important to know about COP 10 in case you ever have to deal with them. Clearly, if you are dealing with COP 10 you have to remember that you are, in effect, dealing with the Inland Revenue.

If the Inland Revenue became suspicious about a stamp duty payment it could result in enquiries being made by COP 10. This is what the tax authorities have to say about linked transactions vis-à-vis stamp duty:

'Section 108 of the Finance Act 2003 states that transactions are regarded as linked if they form part of a single scheme, arrangement or series of transactions between the same vendors(s) and purchaser(s) or parties connected with them. It is a matter of fact whether transactions are linked or not and the parties involved will be the best placed to make that judgment. Transactions do not have to be 'interdependent' in any legal sense in order to be linked. The fact that the

transactions were contemplated at the same time is strong evidence that they are linked.

The way in which the transactions are documented is of much less importance that what precedes the documents. If transactions are negotiated together then this is strong evidence that they are linked. Even if they are negotiated one after the other they could well be linked if, e.g. the fact of the first one has affected the price for the second.

The classic 'non-linked' transaction is the purchase of separate lots at auction. Another example is the renewal of a lease following new negotiations between landlord and tenant. I should say in addition that we do not interpret a 'series of transactions' as just meaning that the transactions follow one after the other (such as the grant of a lease followed by its renewal five years later after new negotiations). They must be connected in some way.

If you are uncertain about the Inland Revenue's interpretation of the law (including its application to a proposed transaction) we [COP 10] *will advise you if your query is in the following categories*

- *the interpretation of legislation passed in the last four Finance Acts ;*
- *the application of double taxation agreements;*
- *whether someone is employed or self employed;*
- *Statements of Practice and extra-statutory concessions;*
- *other areas concerning matters of major public interest in an industry or in the financial sector.*

However, we will not help with tax planning, or advise on transactions designed to avoid or reduce the tax charge which might otherwise be expected to arise. And your query must arise from genuine uncertainty about the meaning of the law.'

This is what it boils down to: whenever you may be selling more than one property to the same Buyer (with or without time gaps) make sure that you 'help' the Buyer pass the *link test* (see Fig. 4 on the next page).

FIG. 4 - THE LINK TEST

No awareness: At the time of sale, the Buyer must not be contemplating buying more than one property (from the same Seller). Equally, the Buyer must not be aware of any other property purchase made in the past (from the same Seller). The Buyer must be able to back this up with crystal clear *documentary* evidence that is irrefutable.

No benefit: No benefit must be derived from a property sale as a result of any other property sale to the same Buyer. The Buyer must be able to back this up with crystal clear documentary evidence that is irrefutable.

If there is awareness but no benefit, it will be regarded as a linked transaction unless the Buyer can clearly prove with documentary evidence that there was no benefit. Even then, the transaction may be regarded as linked by virtue of awareness alone.

If there was benefit but no awareness, it will be regarded as a linked transaction unless the Buyer can clearly prove with documentary evidence that there was no awareness. Even then, the transaction may be regarded as linked by virtue of benefit alone.

If there was no benefit and no awareness it will not be regarded as a linked transaction, but it is still very important for the Buyer to have irrefutable documentary evidence to back this up in case it is queried by the tax authorities.

Note that stamp duty is a self-assessment tax. That is, the Buyer must decide the correct amount of stamp duty to pay, and you do this when filling in the stamp duty payment form. Council tax, for example, is not a self-assessment tax because the tax authorities check your home and then tell you exactly how much tax to pay.

In regard to linked transactions, the following questions come to mind:

1. *If I sell a property (either off-plan or ready built), does that mean I can never again sell another property to the same Buyer without him being penalized with extra stamp duty? The answer is YES unless the Buyer can pass the* **link test** *(see Fig. 5).*

2. *Can I ever sell more than one property to the same Buyer without him being penalized with extra stamp duty? The answer is NO unless the Buyer can pass the* **link test** *(see Fig. 5).*

Section 108 'Linked Transactions' of The Finance Act 2003 is a pointless and pernicious bit of legislation that fully deserves to be abolished. It is pointless because it serves no purpose except to collect more tax. It does not close any so called 'tax loophole' since property transactions that are not linked still get taxed with stamp duty in the usual way. It is pernicious because it serves to castigate bona fide property owners and business people who merely wish to buy more than one property from the same Seller. Furthermore, it goes against a fundamental principle of free enterprise: it discourages repeat business and customer loyalty by imposing tax penalties against this.

Finally, remember that in spite of following the advice in this chapter, it is always necessary for the Inland Revenue to believe you. If they don't you could potentially have an expensive fight on your hands. If you are in any doubt about how to proceed you should consult a solicitor.

Summary of *The Link Strategy For Sellers:*

1. Use this strategy to sell more than one property to the same Buyer without making him pay a higher rate of stamp duty. Do this by helping the Buyer avoid the linked property trap as explained in this chapter. Remember that linkage can apply even if selling properties as separate transactions, with time gaps in between.

2. Use this strategy to build repeat business and customer loyalty with property investors. Do this by helping the Buyer avoid the linked property trap as explained in this chapter.

3. Offer property free of stamp duty without financial loss as a way of generating greater buyer interest and being more successful. Do this by building the cost of stamp duty into the selling price, by using Cash Incentives, and by helping Buyers avoid the linked property trap.

4. Remember that a husband and wife (and close relatives) are regarded as 'connected' and if selling property through both, it will be regarded as a linked transaction.

5. Study the examples given in this chapter to understand how best to help repeat Buyers avoid a linked transaction trap.

6. If you are wanting to sell more than one property to the same buyer and you want to get clarification from the tax authorities so as to avoid linkage before proceeding, be very careful! By discussing the deal with the tax authorities you may no longer be able to help a potential Buyer pass the *link test* for **awareness.**

7. If there is any possibility that you will be selling more than one property to the same Buyer (now or in the future), make sure that you will be able to help the Buyer pass the *link test* (see Fig. 5) by studying this chapter and planning your sales strategy carefully.

Stamp Duty Avoidance Strategy No. 4:

The Price Strategy For Sellers

This strategy will enable a Seller to:

- Offer a property free of stamp duty as a means of attracting interest.

- Get a higher selling price than otherwise.

- Resolve a price impasse, whenever a Seller and Buyer cannot agree a price. Think of the strategy as a way of 'bridging the price gap' whenever a price cannot be agreed.

A Seller would only use *The Price Strategy For Sellers* when:

1. The Buyer and Seller cannot agree a price, or when a Buyer cannot pay the amount wanted by the Seller (for whatever reason).

2. The Buyer is willing to agree a price but cannot afford the mortgage deposit or the buying costs (stamp duty, legal fees, etc).

This is a great strategy for both Sellers and Buyers and will apply to most situations that involve residential property.

At this point you may want to review the chapter titled 'Financial Elements' at the beginning of Part 2 of this book, as we will be referring to these terms in this strategy.

To use this strategy effectively the Seller needs to understand certain mortgage issues faced by the Buyer, even though the Seller may not be involved in any mortgage. Therefore, the explanations that follow take into account certain mortgage issues that apply to the Buyer.

Normally, when a PRICE is agreed between Buyer and Seller, this is the figure that goes on the Buyer's mortgage application form. And provided that the valuation carried out by the Lender is not *less* than the PRICE, the Buyer will get a mortgage based on this figure. To be clear on this important point: **the loan amount is based on the PRICE provided the VALUATION is not lower than the PRICE.**

The Price Strategy For Sellers is based on helping the Buyer get a mortgage based on a *higher* price than the amount actually paid for the property. That way, the buyer ends up with 'cash in hand'.

To explain further we will look at the following example:

EXAMPLE

- Seller's asking price: £210,000 and free of stamp duty.
- Rock bottom amount that Seller is willing to accept: £200,000, but not free of stamp duty.
- Maximum amount that Buyer is willing to pay: £197,000.
- Assumption: Buyer can get a 95% Loan To Value mortgage.
- Deposit is therefore 5%.

Looking at the first aspect of this example, let's consider whether the Seller should offer a property 'free of stamp duty'. Clearly, in doing so, the Seller is undertaking to pay the stamp duty 'on behalf' of the Buyer. To compensate, the Seller can simply increase the selling price by the amount of the stamp duty applicable. This is perfectly legal and many house-building companies do this. For example, in their advertisements, Berkeley Homes offer properties 'Stamp Duty Paid'. There is absolutely no reason why a private Seller cannot do the same, and indeed estate agents are happy to be instructed to do this.

Here are the advantages and disadvantages of offering a property free of stamp duty:

Advantages:

1. Seller gets more market interest because the offer is perceived to be more attractive.

2. Seller can set a price that is close to the stamp duty threshold (e.g. £255,000) without meeting buyer resistance.

3. Seller has greater room for negotiation because the price can be lowered subject to the stamp duty being paid by the Buyer.

4. Seller is able to include the cost of stamp duty in the Buyer's mortgage, thus giving the Buyer another reason for buying the property. This is so because if the price has been increased to take into account the cost of stamp duty, the mortgage will be based on the increased price.

5. Seller has a great bargaining tool: *'If you buy my house you won't have to pay stamp duty'.*

Disadvantages:

1. Seller may meet market resistance to a higher property price that includes the cost of stamp duty.

2. Seller may not be able to offer a competitive price compared to other similar properties being sold nearby.

3. Some Buyers may regard it as a 'sales gimmick' of no significance. Note, however, that this would be wrong. If a Buyer is using a mortgage facility, the mortgage or bank loan will not normally include stamp duty. When the price has the stamp duty factored in, the mortgage will include the cost of the stamp duty.

Tip

Solicitors usually add about £50 - £70 to their conveyancing fees charged to the Buyer for arranging payment of stamp duty. The Seller can save this money for the Buyer by arranging this payment himself. Simply go to http://www.inlandrevenue.gov.uk/so/sdlt_website.htm *and follow the on-screen instructions. Alternatively, telephone the Inland Revenue, 0845 302 1472, and obtain the forms for paying stamp duty by post. Remember to tell your solicitor that you will be arranging the payment of stamp duty through the Buyer. Note that the Buyer will need to sign the form and send a copy to his solicitor as proof of payment (the Seller is not allowed to sign the form as it amounts to a personal declaration of a tax payment). Before you decide what to do, look at a blank form and the guidance notes that come with it.*

Note that when the Seller pays stamp duty, it *must be* paid through the Buyer as only the Buyer (or his solicitor) can sign the stamp duty payment form. So in practice, the Seller would give the stamp duty money to the buyer (either directly or through solicitors) for passing on to the tax authorities.

So should you on balance offer the property free of stamp duty and factor this into the selling price? The answer is generally YES provided that you are not in a *price* competition with a similar property being sold next door. You can, of course, factor in just part of the cost of stamp duty, and round-off the selling price to the nearest one thousand pounds.

> **From now onwards you can always sell a property by offering: 'stamp duty paid'. You can either increase the price to compensate for the cost, absorb the cost yourself, or go half and half.**

Coming back to our example above, we see that there is an impasse: a price cannot be agreed. This is a common occurrence as Sellers often get offers below their asking price. If the Buyer and Seller cannot find common ground, the deal is lost and no sale goes ahead. But using *The Price Strategy For Sellers* this needn't be the case. We will now compare two scenarios based on this example:

Scenario one, based on the *conventional approach*

1. Asking price: £210,000 with no stamp duty to pay (i.e. the Seller pays the stamp duty).

2. Maximum price reduction Seller is willing to go to: £200,000, but Buyer pays stamp duty.

3. Mortgage amount for Buyer would be £190,000 (95% of £200,000).

4. Mortgage Deposit (payment from Buyer to Buyer's Lender) would be: £10,000 (5% of £200,000).

5. Buyer would have to pay **stamp duty**, legal fees, mortgage valuation, and all other costs out of own resources as these cannot be included in the mortgage or property bank loan.

6. Property would be registered at the land registry with a value of £200,000 if sale went ahead.

7. Sale does not go ahead because the maximum amount the Buyer is willing to pay is £197,000.

Scenario two based on *The Price Strategy For Sellers*

1. Asking price: £210,000 with no stamp duty to pay (i.e. the Seller pays the stamp duty).

2. Discounted amount (price agreed after negotiation): £200,000, but Buyer pays stamp duty.

3. Cash Incentive agreed (payment from Seller to Buyer): £10,000 (difference between £210,000 and £200,000, so Seller ends up getting £200,000 for house).

4. Mortgage amount is £199,500 (95% of £210,000).

5. Mortgage Deposit (payment from Buyer to Buyer's Lender): £10,500 (5% of £210,000).

6. Buyer can pay for stamp duty, legal fees, mortgage valuation, and all other costs from the Cash Incentive, and still have thousands of pounds left over.

7. Property is registered at the land registry with a value of £210,000, giving the Buyer more equity.

We will now look at scenario two in more detail and explain the strategy further. What follows is a step by step procedure, including suggested dialogue. There are three steps to follow.

STEP 1: Negotiate a price.

STEP 2: Make an offer.

STEP 3: Confirm it in writing.

STEP 1: Negotiate a price.

- The Seller will naturally negotiate the best price he can get should a Buyer not agree to the asking price. There may come a point when the Seller has to say he will reduce the price provided the Buyer pays the stamp duty. If a price is agreed, that is the end of the matter and you don't go on to steps 2 and 3. If a price cannot be agreed the Seller can use *The Price Strategy For Sellers* to bridge the price gap and clinch a deal that will be good for both the Seller and the Buyer.

- To summarize STEP 1, the Seller will go on to STEP 2 only if the negotiations are not getting anywhere or if the Seller wants to get things moving quickly and reach an agreement.

STEP 2: Make an offer. You go on to this step only if you have not been able to agree a price in the conventional manner. At this point the dialogue and negotiations would go something like this:

Note: Speak slowly when negotiating, don't rush things through. Also, pause after each 'chunk' of dialogue to make sure the Seller has heard you correctly, and make certain there are no misunderstandings. If you get any questions and you don't want to stop at that point, say *'I will go on to explain that in just a moment'.*

- *'I have said that I cannot go below £200,000 and you have said that you cannot offer more than £197,000 and on top of that pay the cost of stamp duty. As we haven't been able to agree a price I would like to make you a special offer that will benefit both of us. It would enable you to buy this house and end up with spare cash to pay for legal fees, stamp duty, and anything else you like. Are you interested?'*

- *'I want to ask you to agree to a selling price of £210,000. Don't worry, you won't actually be paying this price for the house, but the transaction would go through as £210,000.'*

- *'So the price of £210,000 is the price that would go on all the paperwork including your mortgage application. This will be the Open Market Value and the agreed SELLING PRICE between us. As a result, you will get a mortgage based on £210,000 rather than on £197,000. This is a perfectly legal and proper way to proceed. And provided the VALUATION of the house carried out by your Lender is not less than £210,000 you will get your mortgage based on this figure.'*

- *'This means you will get £10,000 more than you need to buy the house. So you get a loan for 210,000, you pay me £200,000, and you have £10,000 left over. This £10,000 is called a Cash Incentive. In practice what would happen is that your solicitor pays my solicitor £210,000 because this is the selling price. Then my solicitor gives my Cash Incentive you via your solicitor. You will be able to use this additional money for anything you like.'*

At this point it is essential to make sure the Buyer understands how the Cash Incentive works. Explain that the Cash Incentive is a payment from the Buyer to himself. But the Cash Incentive money goes to the Buyer *via the Seller*. Fig. 5 on the next page shows the money-flow, step by step:

FIG. 5 - MONEY-FLOW DIAGRAM

Step 1
LENDER
(money loaned to Buyer, based on selling price)

Step 2
BUYER'S SOLICITOR
(Money given to Buyer's solicitor for buying property)

Step 3
SELLER'S SOLICITOR
(Money paid to Seller's solicitor on completion, without deducting the Cash Incentive)

Step 4
BUYER'S SOLICITOR
(Seller's solicitor 'pays' Cash Incentive money to Buyer's solicitor for giving to Buyer)

Step 5
BUYER
Buyer receives Cash Incentive money as part of the final reconciliation of the completion statement prepared by the Buyer's solicitor

To finish this point, explain that the cash incentive is surplus money left over from the mortgage loan (the difference between the amount borrowed and the amount actually paid for the property). The Seller now continues the dialogue to finish the negotiations.

- *'Of course, you will need to tell your solicitor that although you have agreed a PRICE of £210,000, you are only expecting to pay £200,000 because you are getting a £10,000 Cash Incentive from me, the Seller. I'll give you a letter that you can send to your solicitor which explains this.'*

- 'As I said, this is completely legal and above board, and is common practice in the building industry. The £10,000 price difference is called a 'Cash Incentive' and any experienced conveyancer will be familiar with this way of doing business. As mentioned, this £10,000 is a Cash Incentive from me to you but the money does not originate from me – it comes from your own mortgage (from the money you are borrowing to buy this house).'

- 'Have a look at these advertisements. What I am proposing is no different to the way that large building companies operate. You and I are doing the same thing but on a smaller scale. In these advertisements, the building companies are selling direct to buyers just like I am selling direct to you.'

(Show advertisements depicting Cash Incentive offers from builders like Barratt. Answer any remaining questions).

- 'Let's summarize what you get out of the deal:

  1. You get to buy this house (or 'my house') instead of losing it to another Buyer.

  2. You get £10,000 cash-in-hand for spending on anything you like. If you wanted to, this money could finance your mortgage deposit, or be put into a high interest savings account to offset mortgage interest payments. It could certainly be used to pay for legal costs and stamp duty, and enable you to buy this house for little or no money down.

  3. You get to buy a property at below market value (a good bargain). This is so because you're buying a property valued at £210,000 but only paying £200,000.

  4. You get a property with equity, i.e. the potential profit that can be made when re-selling the property. The equity is the difference between the market value and the amount owing on the property. For example, if you are getting a 95% mortgage on £210,000, you will owe 95% of £210,000 which is £199,500. And if the market value is, say £210,000, the equity is £10,500.'

- 'So can I take it that you agree in principle with this strategy? If so, I will give you some information for sending to your solicitor.'

(Wait for Buyer to respond. You need to get a verbal agreement before proceeding).

Summary of the Seller benefits:

1. Seller has found a Buyer and can sell the house.

2. Seller gets to sell the house at the desired price.

3. Seller's house is not devalued in the local market place (this can benefit the Seller if he owns other local properties, or has nearby relatives who own properties).

Summary of the Buyer benefits:

1. Buyer gets a property at below market value (a good bargain).

2. Buyer gets to buy the property at a bargain price because, as a result of getting the Cash Incentive, he paid much less than the registered price.

3. Buyer gets a property with equity, i.e. the potential profit that can be made when re-selling the property.

4. Buyer gets cash (in this example £10,000) that can be used to pay for **stamp duty**, legal fees, conveyancing costs, or just be put into a savings account!). In some cases the savings can be enough for the Buyer to acquire a property with 'no money down'!

TIP

Benefits Sheet

Prepare a sheet of paper that just shows the four Buyer benefits. Use a large size font and use the word 'you' instead of 'Buyer'. Give the *Benefits Sheet* **to the Buyer as you mention these benefits.**

The key to *The Price Strategy For Sellers* is the price difference between the Selling Price you have agreed (and on which the buyer's mortgage is based) and the actual amount paid to the Seller. This difference is the cash incentive (not to be confused with a **'gifted deposit'**) and is common practice in the building industry. Provided the cash incentive is not more than 10% of the

PRICE it will usually not be a cause for concern to anybody. If it is not over 5% (as in this example) it should be perfectly acceptable to all parties. However, 15% cash incentives are not uncommon in the building industry!

Note: The Buyer may declare the *Cash Incentive* on his mortgage application form (there is nothing to hide). The Lender will not mind that the Buyer is getting a Cash Incentive provided the selling price is in line with the valuation report. Remember three things: (i) The *Cash Incentive* is not an additional loan from the Lender, (ii) the Lender is not involved with the Cash Incentive in any direct or legal sense, and (iii) Lenders themselves give Cash Incentives to Buyers (just look at any mortgage magazine).

A Cash Incentive given to a Buyer is not usually regarded as income and is therefore tax free for the Buyer. This is so because the amount is relatively small and is not part of an estate being inherited. The cashback is akin to a gift – if you receive a gift of money it is tax free, like winning the lottery! The only exception to this is a professional property trader. If you are in the business of buying and selling property for a living, then the *Cash Incentive* is regarded as income or profit and is therefore taxable, just like any other earned income. If a *Cash Incentive* is received by a Company, but not a property trading company, it may be taxable depending on the financial situation of the Company, and advice from a tax accountant may be appropriate.

Since the *Cash Incentive* is not a payment for anything, and since the money for the *Cash Incentive* originates from the Lender, the Seller cannot regard it as a loss or as a business expense for accounting purposes.

Regarding Capital Gains Tax, this will not apply if buying or selling your own home (the place where you live). If the property is bought or sold by a property investor, e.g. for re-selling or for buy-to-let, the following applies:

Buyer. If a property is bought at a higher price by virtue of getting a Cash Incentive, the Buyer who is a property trader will pay *less* capital gains tax if and when selling because the price *difference* will be that much less. Note that the capital gains amount is normally based on the difference between the buying price and the selling price as entered at the Land Registry.

Hence, the *Cash Incentive* will ultimately have the effect of reducing the capital gains tax bill. But remember that capital gains tax is not applicable if buying or selling your own home.

Seller. If a property is sold at a higher price by virtue of agreeing to a Cash Incentive, the Seller who is a property investor may pay *more* capital gains tax if and when selling because the price *difference* will be that much more. Note that the capital gains amount is normally based on the difference between the buying price and the selling price as entered at the Land Registry. Hence, the *Cash Incentive* may ultimately have the effect of increasing the capital gains tax bill, assuming the Seller is liable for capital gains tax anyway. There are many ways to avoid or mitigate capital gains tax and therefore a Cash Incentive may little or no effect. But remember that capital gains tax is not applicable if buying or selling your own home.

Important clarification regarding '*gifted deposits*':

- Do not confuse a *Cash Incentive*, as described in this book, with a so called '*gifted deposit*'. Nothing in this book makes use of a *gifted deposit*. In the past, *gifted deposits* were used as a means of getting an amount of money from a Lender that was *higher* than the selling price of the property. However, most Lenders no longer offer 'gifted deposit mortgages'.

- The strategies given in this book do not involve *gifted deposits*. Instead, a Cash Incentive is obtained from the Seller, a transaction that does not involve the Lender. Cash Incentives of this kind are perfectly legal and are widely used by house-building companies.

- A *Cash Incentive* is fundamentally different to a *gifted deposit* because (i) the lender is not involved in the Cash Incentive transaction, and (ii) the mortgage amount is based on the selling price only (with a *gifted deposit* the mortgage amount is based on the sum of the selling price PLUS the *gifted deposit* amount). A Lender is involved with a gifted deposit because the money for the gifted deposit is paid by the Lender to the Buyer, via the solicitor. It is important to make sure your solicitor understands the difference, and that you are not proposing to get involved with any kind of *gifted deposit*.

- Lenders are phasing out *gifted deposits* (even though they are legal) because 'mission creep' has set in. That is, the amount of the *gifted deposit* requested by borrowers (in addition to the loan amount to buy the property) was going up to 15%, 20%, and even 25% of the property value. As a result, some Buyers ended up taking on mortgage debts that they could not afford to repay. The tabloid press had a field day blaming Lenders for lending too much money to 'vulnerable' people.

- The *Cash Incentive* strategies proposed in this book are different because the Lenders are not involved in the process. The *Cash Incentive* is a private arrangement between the Buyer and the Seller (albeit through solicitors), and provided the mortgage is based on the SELLING PRICE and VALUATION, there can be no objections from any of the parties involved.

To reassure the Buyer about this way of doing business, explain that virtually all house building companies operate this way. Show the Buyer some typical advertisements such as the following:

A. Advertisement extract from Kingsoak Homes: *'Options include 5% deposit paid, up to £10,000 cashback, stamp duty paid, home exchange, investor package'.*

B. Advertisement extract from Barratt Homes: *'Purchase plans include home exchange, 5 % deposit paid, stamp duty paid, £5,000 cashback, investor package'.*

An examination of the Barratt advertisement shows the following: Barratt is the Seller. So when a house is bought from Barratt the Buyer gets a sum of money, i.e. a Cash Incentive. In this example, the Cash Incentive takes the form of a 5% deposit payment, a **stamp duty** payment, £5,000 cash, and so on. In other words, Barratt is giving the Buyer a sum of money (financial package) as a reward for buying its property.

Note that Barratt has factored the cost of the Cash Incentive into its selling price, and that the Buyer will be getting a mortgage based on this selling price.

The Price Strategy For Sellers uses the same strategy employed by Barratt and many other property builders. In the example at the beginning of this chapter, you are 'giving' the Buyer, a £10,000 Cash Incentive in return for buying your property.

There is absolutely nothing underhand about this strategy – it is perfectly legal and proper. Private individuals have the same right to use this strategy as much as house-building companies do. So when you meet a Buyer who tries to negotiate a lower price, do your best to agree a price. But if a price cannot be agreed and there is a price gap to bridge, use *The Price Strategy For Sellers* and show the Buyer some Cash Incentive advertisements from builders such as Barratt.

Make sure that you brief your solicitor about your intention to offer a 'Cash Incentive' should it be necessary in your negotiations. Do this before putting your property on the market. If your solicitor is not familiar with the concept of a 'Cash Incentive' in a property transaction you should perhaps find another solicitor. Then, if a Buyer needs reassurance about the strategy, you can tell the Buyer to ask his solicitor to contact your solicitor to get confirmation that a Cash Incentive is a perfectly acceptable way of proceeding.

STEP 3: Confirm it in writing.

Let's recap. In step 1 you negotiated the best price possible in the conventional manner but you were unable to agree a selling price with the Buyer. In step 2 you made an offer based on *The Price Strategy For Sellers* and you got a positive response indicating cooperation with the strategy. Now, in step 3 you will be giving the Buyer two letters.

The first letter is a written confirmation from you to the Buyer to clarify the offer you have just made. This first letter would be issued in duplicate so that the Buyer can sign and return one copy to indicate an agreement in principle to proceed. Try to get the letter signed there and then (otherwise it can be posted to you).

The second letter is a draft letter for the Buyer to send to his solicitor to get things moving. Both these letters are shown below, with suggested wording that can be adapted as necessary.

Note: These two letters would also be copied to any estate agent that may be involved in the transaction.

Price confirmation letter from Seller to Buyer

(date)

From: (Seller's name and address)

To: (Buyer's name and address)

Re: Sale of my property (enter property address)

Following our meeting, I confirm that we have agreed in principle the following price details for the sale of my house:

SELLING PRICE: (Price agreed for selling property)	£ (enter agreed price) [Note: In the case of the above example, this would be £210,000]
*Less Cash Incentive to buyer: (For redecoration, repairs, and miscellaneous costs)	£ (enter agreed amount) [Note: In the case of the above example, this would be £10,000]
Total cash on completion:	£ (enter difference of above two figures) [Note: In the case of the above example, this would be £200,000]

*The Cash Incentive referred to above is a sum of money that will be paid from the Seller's solicitor to the Buyer's solicitor on completion of the property transaction.

The address of my solicitor is as follows: (enter Seller's solicitor details).

I confirm that the Buyer will declare the Cash Incentive on his mortgage application form. (Delete this paragraph if Buyer is not using a loan to buy the property).

It is understood that the sale of my house is subject to contract, and a satisfactory valuation if it is being bought with a mortgage. The next step is to tell your solicitor to buy this property from me as detailed above.

[THE FOLLOWING PARAGRAPH APPLIES ONLY IF AN ESTATE AGENT IS INVOLVED]:

I confirm I will ask my estate agent to issue a *'memorandum of sale'* and withdraw the property from the market. I will make clear to the estate agent that the SELLING PRICE is the amount *before* the Cash Incentive (not the discounted amount). I will ask the estate agent to send a copy of the *memorandum of sale* to you so that you can ask your Lender to carry out the mortgage valuation of my property. Please sign the declaration below and give me a copy of this letter to indicate that you agree in principle to buy my property as explained above. I will then be able to withdraw the property from the market.

[THE FOLLOWING PARAGRAPH APPLIES ONLY IF AN ESTATE AGENT IS **NOT** INVOLVED]:

As no estate agent is involved in this transaction, this letter takes the place of the *memorandum of sale.* Please sign the declaration below and give me a copy of this letter to indicate that you agree in principle to buy my property as explained above. I will then be able to withdraw the property from the market.

If anything is not clear please contact me at any time.

Yours sincerely,

(enter Seller's name)

DECLARATION BY BUYER: I agree in principle to BUY your property on the terms described above, subject to valuation and subject to contract.

Signed: ....Date:..................

Print Name: ....

You should give the Buyer two copies of the above letter so that one copy can be signed and returned to you. You should then help the Buyer further by giving him a draft letter for sending to his solicitor. Here is the wording:

Letter from Buyer to Buyer's solicitor

Dear (Solicitor)

Property: (Address)

I have asked you to act for me in the purchase of a property. I am now writing to explain that I wish to buy the above named property and the details are as follows:

1. Name of Seller: (enter name).

2. Seller's solicitor: (enter name, address, and telephone number).

3. Price for buying property: (enter SELLING PRICE, not discounted amount).

4. Cash Incentive: I have also agreed to receive a Cash Incentive of £ (enter amount). This sum of money is to be paid to me upon completion, from the mortgage amount that I will be borrowing.

I confirm that I will declare the Cash Incentive on my mortgage application form. (Delete this paragraph if Buyer is not using a loan to buy the property).

Please find enclosed a copy of a price confirmation letter I have received from the Seller.

Yours sincerely

(name of Buyer)

The above letter from the Buyer to his solicitor is important as it will focus the Buyer's mind into taking the correct action and being committed to following the strategy.

If the Buyer will not sign the declaration in the letter there and then, you should allow the Buyer to take the letter away, and consult their solicitor should they wish to. In this event, you should make it clear that you cannot take the property off the market until the letter is signed or until you get a clear indication of an intention to buy.

Important Note: When mentioning this strategy to a solicitor, only talk in terms of giving a Cash Incentive to the Buyer. Do not talk in terms of giving a cashback that is deducted from the Buyer's mortgage money, as this is not the case, and solicitors may regard this as somewhat dubious. Also, point out that the Buyer will be declaring the cash incentive on the mortgage application form, and that this is no different to the Cash Incentives given by house-building companies, a practice that is common all over the UK.

The Price Strategy For Sellers then, is using the Buyer's mortgage company to in effect give the Buyer cash in hand. In doing this, the Buyer is able to buy the Seller's property at a higher price than otherwise. From the Buyer's point of view, it is much better to end up with a mortgage of £199,500 and have £10,000 cash in hand, than to end up with a mortgage of £190,000 and no cash in hand.

The Buyer may end up paying a little more in monthly interest on a mortgage of £199,500 compared to £190,000, but the difference is negligible. For example, if the mortgage interest is, say, 5% the monthly payment would be about £831 compared to £792 (a difference of about £39). And remember, the Buyer doesn't have to spend all of the Cash Incentive – he can, if he wants to, put some of the Cash Incentive money into a high-interest savings account to offset the small increase in monthly interest.

Or the Buyer could use any money remaining from the Cash Incentive to reduce his mortgage. He could even factor the Cash Incentive into the mortgage deposit, thus reducing the amount to pay as a deposit. The main advantage is of course the fact that he has £10,000 cash in hand (in this example) at a time when he most needs it.

If a Buyer is buying his home with limited savings and limited income, a Cash Incentive can sometimes make or break a property deal. For the Buyer, **The Price Strategy For Sellers** will improve cash flow, particularly if a buy-to-let property is involved. In this scenario, the Buyer's small increase in monthly interest will not matter as much since he gets tax relief on mortgage interest.

The Big Question

How does the Seller persuade the Buyer to get a bigger mortgage as a means of getting a Cash Incentive (and pay more for the property)? After all, that is what *The Price Strategy For Sellers* is all about. This is how:

Step one: Set Realistic Open Market Value.

- Before putting the property up for sale establish a realistic **open market value** for your property. Then base your selling price on this. Do this by talking to estate agents or by checking the prices of similar properties in the area. Then set your asking price to include the cost of stamp duty. Either decide that you will absorb this cost, or put the price up to compensate for this cost (or do 'half and half').

- Including stamp duty in the price of a house is a good way of attracting interest and it will make your offer stand out from the other properties in the area. If you are using an estate agent they can make your property stand out from the others by featuring the free stamp duty. Clearly, if you put the price up to include the stamp duty, the Buyer will in effect end up paying this cost. But, by doing this, the Buyer will be able to pay the stamp duty using *mortgage money* instead of his own money.

TIP

Offering to sell a property free of stamp duty is a good marketing strategy. But to do this you must decide whether to put the price up to compensate for the cost of stamp duty, or whether to absorb the cost yourself as a way of generating greater buyer interest. Although it is generally a good thing to do, there is no clear-cut answer to this as it depends on local property market conditions and your personal circumstances. If you are selling through an estate agent, get their advice on this matter.

146

- Establish your minimum price: have a clear figure in mind and make this your rock bottom price below which you will not sell. This figure should not include the cost of stamp duty. Your objective is to get your asking price or a price between your asking price and your minimum price. If a buyer will not meet your minimum price, you would then use *The Price Strategy For Sellers.*

Step two: Be flexible on price.

Make it clear to all and sundry (potential buyers, advertisements, estate agents, leaflets, etc) that you will accept offers, or that you can be flexible on the price. The abbreviation O.N.O. (Or Near Offer) can be used when stating the price. You want a Buyer to be willing to negotiate with you because you can then use *The Price Strategy For Sellers* if a deal cannot be agreed.

Step three: Be prepared.

Make sure you are prepared with all the paperwork that you need. Prepare a folder containing all the documents relating to *The Price Strategy For Sellers.* These are:

1. The Buyer benefits sheet.
2. Money-flow diagram (see Fig. 5 in this chapter).
3. Samples of house-building company advertisements showing Cash Incentive offers (check property newspapers, magazines, etc).
4. Price confirmation letter from Seller to Buyer.
5. Letter from Buyer to Buyer's solicitor.

Step four: Use the Strategy.

Apply *The Price Strategy For Sellers* exactly as explained in this chapter. Point out the benefits to the Buyer. These are genuine benefits – it's a 'win, win' solution for both the Buyer and the Seller. Remember: Use the strategy as a last resort. *Do not use the strategy if a price can be agreed in the conventional manner.* But note the following: If a buyer says he is willing to agree the price but does not have enough ready cash to pay for the mortgage deposit, the **stamp duty**, the legal fees, etc. then consider proposing *The Price Strategy For Sellers* to make it possible for the Buyer to do business with you.

Combining Two Amounts

You can combine the discount amount and the stamp duty amount to give the Buyer a bigger Cash Incentive than otherwise (with no loss to the Seller). .

To clarify this further, here is an example:

1. The asking price is £210,000.

2. **Discount amount £5,000.** After negotiation you agree a price reduction of £5,000, bringing the price down to £205,000.

3. **Stamp duty amount £2,000.** The stamp duty on £210,000 at 1% is £2,100, so the Seller can increase the selling price by, say £2,000 (from £210,000 to £212,000).

4. The Seller can then offer a Cash Incentive of £7,000 (the total of the discount amount of £5,000 and the stamp duty amount of £2,000).

5. The Seller gets paid the agreed £205,000 and the Buyer gets a mortgage based on £212,000 with a Cash Incentive of £7,000.

Most property transactions are likely to involve combining two amounts in this way, to give as big a Cash Incentive as possible. These two amounts are: (i) the difference between the asking price and the reduced price negotiated, and (ii) the difference between the asking price and a higher price based on adding the stamp duty.

When these two elements (the discount amount and the stamp duty amount) are combined, this makes for a very powerful and effective strategy. Remember that a big Cash Incentive for the buyer means that the Seller can offer or negotiate better terms.

Summary of *The Price Strategy For Sellers:*

1. Brief your solicitor about the use of a *'Cash Incentive'* for selling your property. Say that you may offer a Cash Incentive to a Buyer if you cannot get the asking price. You should not need to explain the whole strategy. If the solicitor is not familiar with the concept of a *'Cash Incentive' as part of a property transaction* find another solicitor. The purpose here is to 'prime' your solicitor to be receptive and to fully co-operate with the Buyer's solicitor when the time comes. Any experienced conveyancer will be familiar with the concept of a Cash Incentive.

2. Use *The Price Strategy For Sellers* as a last resort (i.e. when the price required cannot be obtained). Follow the step-by-step procedure in this chapter and have to hand the following: (i) The Buyer benefits sheet, (ii) Money-flow diagram, (iii) Samples of building company advertisements showing Cash Incentive offers, (iv) Price confirmation letter from Seller to Buyer – two copies, (v) Letter from Buyer to Buyer's solicitor.

3. Show the Buyer several advertisements used by building companies such as Barratt, offering Cash Incentives in the form of stamp duty payments, and so on. Explain that what you are proposing is no different to the way that large building companies operate, but on a smaller scale. Explain that a Cash Incentive in the building industry is a perfectly legal and usual way of doing business.

4. Show the Buyer a diagram of the money flow (see Fig. 5) to make absolutely sure that the buyer understands what is being proposed.

5. Make full use of a combined strategy to offer as big a Cash Incentive as possible. Do this by combining the discount amount with the stamp duty amount. That way you will always be able to offer a Cash Incentive, even when little or no price reduction can be offered.

6. Agree the strategy with the Buyer. If necessary say: *'Will you agree to buy my house based on a selling price of £XYZ and a Cash Incentive to you of £ABC?'* When the buyer agrees or shows serious interest, give him the two letter documents.

7. Point out that you cannot take the property off the market until the Buyer signs the declaration on the price confirmation letter to indicate an agreement in principle. Make sure you get a copy of the signed letter.

8. Follow through with all parties (Buyer, Estate Agent, and Solicitor) to get things moving.

The Valuation Strategy For Sellers

This strategy will enable a Seller to:

- Offer a property free of stamp duty as a means of attracting interest.

- Get a higher selling price than otherwise.

- Resolve a price impasse, whenever a Seller and Buyer cannot agree a price. Think of the strategy as a way of 'bridging the price gap' whenever a price cannot be agreed.

A Seller would only use *The Valuation Strategy For Sellers* when:

1. The Buyer and Seller cannot agree a price, or when a Buyer (for whatever reason) cannot pay the amount wanted by the Seller.

2. The Buyer is willing to agree a price but cannot afford the mortgage deposit or the buying costs (stamp duty, legal fees, etc).

This is a great strategy for both Sellers and Buyers and will apply to most situations that involve residential property.

Even though the Seller is not involved in the Buyer's mortgage, the Seller needs to understand certain mortgage issues faced by the Buyer, to take full advantage of the strategy.

Normally, when a PRICE is agreed between Buyer and Seller, this is the figure that goes on the Buyer's mortgage application form. And provided that the valuation carried out by the Lender is not *less* than the PRICE, the Buyer will get a mortgage based on this figure. To be clear then: **the loan amount is based on the SELLING PRICE, provided the VALUATION is not lower than the PRICE.**

The Valuation Strategy For Sellers is based on helping the Buyer get a mortgage based on a *higher* amount than the amount *actually paid* for the property. That way, the buyer ends up with 'cash in hand'.

So by helping the Buyer get a bigger mortgage than otherwise *The Valuation Strategy For Sellers* helps the Seller to sell a property more quickly and profitably.

This strategy is a 'win, win' situation for all concerned, and as you will see, it is a strategy that should be applied to virtually any property transaction, whether buying or selling.

How can the Seller help the Buyer get a bigger mortgage than otherwise? The strategy is based on the principle of getting a full market valuation for the property (the higher the valuation the better). A good (i.e. high) valuation will result in a more favourable loan for the Buyer, which in turn will benefit the seller. Let's briefly look at the financial elements that go into this strategy.

PRICE. This is the 'official' SELLING PRICE. Normally, when a PRICE is agreed between Buyer and Seller, this is the figure that goes on the Buyer's mortgage application form. And provided that the valuation carried out by the LENDER is not *less* than the PRICE, the Buyer will get a mortgage based on this figure.

AMOUNT PAID. This is the reduced price that has been negotiated and agreed. It is the actual amount of money that the Seller will end up getting for the property. Note that the LOAN is based on the PRICE (not the AMOUNT PAID), provided the VALUATION is not lower than the PRICE.

152

VALUATION. This is the open market value deemed to apply to the property by the LENDER. So here, we are not talking about a valuation carried out by an estate agent or anybody else, unless employed by the LENDER to do the valuation. It is based on the resell value (not the cost of rebuilding). Should the property be repossessed, the LENDER wants to know it will be able to get its money back by reselling the property.

LENDER. The mortgage company or bank that is lending money to the Buyer as a secured loan, i.e. the loan is secured on the property.

COMPARABLE. This is short for 'comparable price'. It refers to another property near the one being sold, that is similar in type and price. So if you have three comparables, it means you have information on three other properties that can be compared to the property you are buying or selling in terms of price and type of property. Comparables do not have to be physically identical to the property being sold, just roughly similar, so that like is being compared with like.

Coming back to the VALUATION, the sequence of events leading up to this event is as follows:

1. The Buyer finds a property he wants to buy.

2. He agrees a price with the Seller.

3. The Seller and Buyer instruct solicitors.

4. The Buyer applies for a mortgage (and pays the mortgage company to carry out a valuation).

5. The mortgage company instructs a Valuer to carry out a valuation.

6. If the valuation is satisfactory (i.e. not lower than the PRICE) a mortgage is granted.

The Valuation Strategy For Sellers involves getting as high a valuation as possible so as to fully reflect the open market value of the property. This is perfectly legal and proper as no misrepresentation of the value is involved.

The following example explains the strategy further:

EXAMPLE

- Seller's asking price: £230,000.

- Rock bottom amount that Seller is willing to accept after negotiation: £228,000.

- Buyer is only able to offer £224,000, so there is a £4,000 price gap that is preventing the sale from going ahead.

- For this example we assume a valuation of £238,000.

- Buyer can get a 95% Loan To Value mortgage.

- Deposit is therefore 5%.

In this example we will compare two scenarios:

Scenario one, based on the *conventional sales approach*

1. Original asking price: £230,000

2. Price reduction that Seller is willing to give: £228,000 (Buyer can only afford £224,000).

3. Selling price that would be agreed if Buyer were to proceed: £228,000

4. Amount that would be paid to Seller on completion if Buyer able to buy: £228,000.

5. Mortgage amount would be £216,600 (95% of £228,000).

6. Mortgage Deposit (payment from Buyer to Buyer's Lender) would be: £11,400 (5% of £228,000).

7. Buyer would have to pay for stamp duty, legal fees, mortgage valuation, and all other costs out of own resources as these cannot be included in the mortgage or property bank loan.

8. Property would be registered at the land registry with a value of £228,000.

9. In this scenario the sale would be lost unless the Seller or Buyer was willing to close the £4,000 price gap.

Scenario two based on *The Valuation Strategy For Sellers*

1. Original asking price: £230,000

2. Price reduction that Seller is willing to give: £228,000 (Buyer can only afford £224,000).

3. Selling price agreed: £238,000 (£10,000 more than the amount to be paid for house).

4. Amount paid to Seller on completion: £238,000 (£10,000 more than the amount agreed for house).

5. Cash Incentive agreed (payment from Seller to Buyer): £10,000 (difference between £238,000 and £228,000, so Seller ends up getting £228,000 for house).

6. Mortgage amount is £226,100 (95% of £238,000).

7. Mortgage Deposit (payment from Buyer to Buyer's Lender): £11,900 (5% of £238,000).

8. Buyer can pay for stamp duty, legal fees, mortgage valuation, and all other costs from the £10,000 Cash Incentive, and still have money left over. Alternatively, the Cash Incentive can finance the mortgage deposit (the Buyer may need to get a two- to three-day bridging loan if he has no savings).

9. Property is registered at the land registry with a value of £238,000.

10. In this scenario the sale goes through because the Seller ends up with £228,000 and the Buyer gets a £10,000 Cash Incentive (and is not short of money!).

We will now look at scenario two in more detail and explain the strategy further. What follows is a step by step procedure, including suggested dialogue.

STEP 1: Negotiate a price.

STEP 2: Make an offer.

STEP 3: Confirm it in writing.

STEP 1: Negotiate a price. The Buyer and Seller will negotiate a price in the conventional manner. It is assumed in this example that a price reduction of £2,000 was offered by the Seller but it could not be accepted. The Seller will now move onto STEP 2 and apply *The Valuation Strategy For Sellers* to bridge the price gap.

STEP 2: Make an offer. As the Seller is in danger of losing the opportunity to sell the house there is nothing to lose by making a special proposal to the Buyer. This proposal will enable the house to be sold at £228,000, plus giving the Buyer cash to pay for **stamp duty** and other legal costs. The dialogue would go along the lines that follow.

Note: Speak slowly when negotiating, don't rush things through. Also, pause after each 'chunk' of dialogue to make sure the Seller has heard you correctly, and make certain there are no misunderstandings. If you get any questions and you don't want to stop at that point, say *'I will go on to explain that in just a moment'.*

Dialogue:

- *'I have offered to reduce the price to £228,000 and you have told me that the maximum you can pay is £224,000. As we have a price gap of £4,000 I would like to make a special proposal that will help both of us in this situation. Can I explain this to you?'*

- *'Okay, what I would like to propose is that we agree on a selling price of £238,000. In this situation, you would get a mortgage based on £238,000, but you would only pay me £228,000. That would leave you with £10,000 cash in hand.'*

  Note that you will have arrived at a figure of £238,000 having researched the values of similar properties in the area - more on this later.

- *'The price of £238,000 is the price that would go on all the paperwork including your mortgage application. This will help you to cover the costs you will incur in buying my house (legal fees, stamp duty, etc).'*

- *'In effect, you would be getting a mortgage or bank loan for £10,000 more than you need to buy this house. So on completion, your solicitor will give my solicitor the £238,000 as being the selling price for the house. Immediately afterwards, my solicitor will then give your solicitor a £10,000 Cash Incentive for giving to you. Of course, we will both need to tell our solicitors to do this, and I will confirm all of this in writing.'*

- *'Everything we have discussed is completely legal and above board, and is common practice throughout the building industry. The £10,000 price difference is called a 'Cash Incentive' and any experienced conveyancer will be familiar with this way of doing business. This £10,000 is a Cash Incentive from me to you but the money does not come from me – it comes from your own mortgage (from the money you are borrowing to buy my house).'*

At this point it is essential to make sure the Buyer understands how the Cash Incentive works. Explain that the Cash Incentive is a payment from the Buyer to himself. But the Cash Incentive money goes to the Buyer *via the Seller*. Fig. 6 on the next page shows the money-flow, step by step:

FIG. 6 - MONEY-FLOW DIAGRAM

Step 1

LENDER

(money loaned to Buyer, based on selling price)

Step 2

BUYER'S SOLICITOR

(Money given to Buyer's solicitor for buying property)

Step 3

SELLER'S SOLICITOR

(Money paid to Seller's solicitor on completion, without deducting the Cash Incentive)

Step 4

BUYER'S SOLICITOR

(Seller's solicitor 'pays' Cash Incentive money to Buyer's solicitor for giving to Buyer)

Step 5

BUYER

Buyer receives Cash Incentive money as part of the final reconciliation of the completion statement prepared by the Buyer's solicitor

---

To finish this point, explain that the cash incentive amounts to surplus money left over from the mortgage loan (the difference between the amount borrowed and the amount actually paid for the property). The Seller now continues the dialogue to finish the negotiations.

- *'Have a look at these advertisements. What I am proposing is no different to the way that large building companies operate, but on a smaller scale. In these advertisements, the building companies are selling direct to buyers, just as I am selling direct to you.'*

(Show advertisements depicting Cash Incentive offers from builders like Barratt. Answer any questions).

- *'Let's summarize what you get out of the deal:*

  1. *You get to buy this house instead of losing it to another Buyer.*

  2. *You get £10,000 cash in hand for spending on anything you like. If you wanted to, this money could finance your mortgage deposit, or be put into a high interest savings account to offset mortgage interest payments. It could certainly be used to pay for legal costs and stamp duty, and enable you to buy this house for little or no money down.*

  3. *You get to buy a property at below market value (a good bargain). This is so because you're buying a property valued at £238,000 but only paying £228,000.*

  4. *You get a property with equity, i.e. the potential profit that can be made when reselling the property. The equity is the difference between the market value and the amount owing on the property. For example, if you are getting a 95% mortgage on £238,000, you will owe £226,100. And if the market value is, say £238,000, the equity is £11,900.*

  5. *You get the Cash Incentive as partly interest-free money if the property is a 'buy-to-let'. This is so because you get tax relief on mortgage interest.'*

(Give the Buyer a separate sheet of paper with a list of the benefits. Answer any questions).

- *'So can I take it that you agree in principle with this strategy? If so, I will give you some information for sending to your solicitor.'*

The benefits to the Buyer are:

1. Buyer is able to buy the property instead of losing it.

2. Buyer gets a property at below market value (a good bargain) because the amount actually paid for the property is less than the open market value.

3. Buyer gets a property with equity, i.e. the potential profit that can be made when reselling the property.

4. Buyer gets cash (in this example £10,000) that can be used to pay for stamp duty, legal fees, conveyancing costs, or just be put into a savings account!).

5. Buyer gets the Cash Incentive as partly interest-free money if the property is a 'buy-to-let'. This is so because the Buyer gets tax relief on mortgage interest.

The benefits to the Seller are:

1. Seller has found a Buyer and can sell the house.

2. Seller gets to sell the house at the required price (in this example a price gap of £4,000 has been bridged by the Buyer's own finance).

3. Seller's house is not devalued in the local market place (this can benefit the Seller if he/she owns other local properties, or has nearby relatives who own properties).

The key to *The Valuation Strategy For Sellers* is the price difference between the agreed selling price on which the mortgage is based and the actual amount paid to the Seller. This difference is known in the trade as a 'Cash Incentive' (not to be confused with a *'gifted deposit'*) and is common practice in the building industry. Provided the Cash Incentive is not more than 10% of the PRICE it will usually not be a cause for concern to anybody. If it is not over 5% (as in this example) it should be perfectly acceptable to all parties. However, Cash Incentives of 15% are not uncommon in the building industry!

Note: The Buyer may declare the *Cash Incentive* on his mortgage application form (there is nothing to hide). The Lender will not mind that the Buyer is getting a Cash Incentive provided the selling price is in line with the valuation report. Remember three things: (i) The *Cash Incentive* is not an additional loan from the Lender, (ii) the Lender is not involved with the Cash Incentive in any direct or legal sense, and (iii) Lenders themselves give Cash Incentives to Buyers (just look at any mortgage magazine).

A Cash Incentive given to a Buyer is not usually regarded as income and is therefore tax free for the Buyer. This is so because the amount is relatively small and is not part of an estate being

160

inherited. The cashback is akin to a gift – if you receive a gift of money it is tax free, like winning the lottery! The only exception to this is a professional property trader. If you are in the business of buying and selling property for a living, then the *Cash Incentive* is regarded as income or profit and is therefore taxable, just like any other earned income. If a *Cash Incentive* is received by a Company, but not a property trading company, it may be taxable depending on the financial situation of the Company, and advice from a tax accountant may be appropriate.

Since the *Cash Incentive* is not a payment for anything, and since the money for the *Cash Incentive* originates from the Lender, the Seller cannot regard it as a loss or as a business expense for accounting purposes.

Regarding Capital Gains Tax, this will not apply if buying or selling your own home (the place where you live). If the property is bought or sold by a property trader/investor, e.g. for reselling or for buy-to-let, the following applies:

Buyer. If a property is bought at a higher price by virtue of getting a Cash Incentive, the Buyer who is a property investor will pay *less* capital gains tax if and when selling because the price *difference* will be that much less. Note that the capital gains amount is normally based on the difference between the buying price and the selling price as entered at the Land Registry. Hence, the *Cash Incentive* will ultimately have the effect of reducing the capital gains tax bill. But remember that capital gains tax is not applicable if buying or selling your own home.

Seller. If a property is sold at a higher price by virtue of agreeing to a Cash Incentive, the Seller who is a property investor may pay *more* capital gains tax if and when selling because the price *difference* will be that much more. Note that the capital gains amount is normally based on the difference between the buying price and the selling price as entered at the Land Registry. Hence, the *Cash Incentive* may ultimately have the effect of increasing the capital gains tax bill, assuming the Seller is liable for capital gains tax anyway. There are many ways to avoid or mitigate capital gains tax and therefore a Cash Incentive may have little or no effect. But remember that capital gains tax is not applicable if buying or selling your own home.

Important clarification regarding *'gifted deposits'*:

- Do not confuse a *Cash Incentive*, as described in this book, with a so called *'gifted deposit'*. Nothing in this book makes use of a *gifted deposit*. In the past, *gifted deposits* were used as a means of getting an amount of money from a Lender that was *higher* than the selling price of the property. However, most Lenders no longer offer 'gifted deposit mortgages'.

- The strategies given in this book do not involve *gifted deposits*. Instead, a Cash Incentive is obtained from the Seller, a transaction that does not involve the Lender. Cash Incentives of this kind are perfectly legal and are widely used by house-building companies.

- A *Cash Incentive* is fundamentally different to a *gifted deposit* because (i) the lender is not involved in the Cash Incentive transaction, and (ii) the mortgage amount is based on the selling price only (with a *gifted deposit* the mortgage amount is based on the sum of the selling price PLUS the *gifted deposit* amount). A Lender is involved with a gifted deposit because the money for the gifted deposit is paid by the Lender to the Buyer, via the solicitor. It is important to make sure your solicitor understands the difference, and that you are not proposing to get involved with any kind of *gifted deposit*.

- Lenders are phasing out *gifted deposits* (even though they are legal) because 'mission creep' has set in. That is, the amount of the *gifted deposit* requested by borrowers (in addition to the loan amount to buy the property) was going up to 15%, 20%, and even 25% of the property value. As a result, some Buyers ended up taking on mortgage debts that they could not afford to repay. The tabloid press had a field day blaming Lenders for lending too much money to 'vulnerable' people.

- The *Cash Incentive* strategies proposed in this book are different because the Lenders are not involved in the process. The *Cash Incentive* is a private arrangement between the Buyer and the Seller (albeit through solicitors), and provided the mortgage is based on the SELLING PRICE and VALUATION, there can be no objections from any of the parties involved.

To reassure the Buyer about this way of doing business, explain that virtually all house building companies operate this way. Show the Buyer some typical advertisements such as the following:

162

A. Advertisement extract from Kingsoak Homes: *'Options include 5% deposit paid, up to £10,000 Cash Incentive, stamp duty paid, home exchange, investor package'.*

B. Advertisement extract from Barratt Homes: *'Purchase plans include home exchange, 5 % deposit paid, stamp duty paid, £5,000 cashback, investor package'.*

An examination of the Barratt advertisement shows the following: Barratt is the Seller. So when a house is bought from Barratt, the Buyer gets a sum of money (i.e. a 'Cash Incentive'). In this example, the Cash Incentive takes the form of a 5% deposit payment, a **stamp duty** payment, £5,000 cash, and so on. In other words, Barratt is giving the Buyer a sum of money (financial package) as a reward for buying its property.

Note that Barratt has factored the cost of the Cash Incentive into its selling price, and that the Buyer will be getting a mortgage based on this selling price.

The Valuation Strategy For Sellers uses the same strategy employed by Barratt and many other property builders. In our example, you are 'giving' the Buyer a £10,000 Cash Incentive in return for buying your property.

So when you apply *The Valuation Strategy For Sellers* you are, in effect, enabling the Buyer to enjoy the same kind of benefits that building companies give to their clients. There is absolutely nothing underhand about this strategy – it is perfectly legal and proper. Private individuals have the same right to use this strategy as much as house-building companies do. So when you meet a Buyer to negotiate a price, be equipped with advertisements from builders such as Barratt.

Before putting the property up for sale, brief your solicitor about your intentions to offer a *Cash Incentive* to a Buyer if a price cannot be reached. If your solicitor is not familiar with the concept of a *Cash Incentive* in a property transaction you should perhaps find another solicitor. Then, should the Buyer wish to, he can ask his solicitor to contact your solicitor to get confirmation that a Cash Incentive is a perfectly acceptable way of proceeding.

STEP 3: Confirm it in writing.

Let's recap. In step 1 you negotiated the best price possible in the usual manner but you were unable to agree a selling price with the Buyer. In step 2 you made an offer based on *The Valuation Strategy For Sellers* and you got a positive response indicating co-operation with the strategy. Now, in step 3 you will be giving the Buyer two letters.

The first letter is a written confirmation from you to the Buyer to clarify the offer you have just made. This first letter would be issued in duplicate so that the Buyer can sign and return one copy to indicate an agreement in principle to proceed. Try to get the letter signed there and then (otherwise it can be posted to you).

The second letter is a draft letter for the Buyer to send to his solicitor to get things moving. Both these letters are shown below, with suggested wording that can be adapted as necessary.

Note: These two letters would also be copied to any estate agent that may be involved in the transaction.

Price confirmation letter from Seller to Buyer

(date)

From: (Seller's name and address)

To: (Buyer's name and address)

Re: Sale of my property (enter property address)

Following our meeting, I confirm that we have agreed in principle the following price details for the sale of my house:

SELLING PRICE: (Price agreed for selling property)	£ (enter agreed price) [Note: In the case of the above example, this would be £238,000]
*Less Cash Incentive to buyer: (For redecoration, repairs, and miscellaneous costs)	£ (enter agreed amount) [Note: In the case of the above example, this would be £10,000]
Total cash on completion:	£ (enter difference of above two figures) [Note: In the case of the above example, this would be £228,000]

*The Cash Incentive referred to above is a sum of money that will be paid from the Seller's solicitor to the Buyer's solicitor on completion of the property transaction.

The address of my solicitor is as follows: (enter Seller's solicitor details).

I confirm that the Buyer will declare the cash incentive on his mortgage application form. (Delete this paragraph if Buyer is not using a loan to buy the property).

It is understood that the sale of my house is subject to contract and a satisfactory valuation if it is being bought with a mortgage. The next step is to tell your solicitor to buy this property from me as detailed above.

[THE FOLLOWING PARAGRAPH APPLIES ONLY IF AN ESTATE AGENT IS INVOLVED]:

I confirm I will ask my estate agent to issue a '*memorandum of sale*' and withdraw the property from the market. I will make clear to the estate agent that the SELLING PRICE is the amount *before* the Cash Incentive (not the discounted amount). I will ask the estate agent to send a copy of the *memorandum of sale* to you so that you can ask your Lender to carry out the mortgage valuation of my property. Please sign the declaration below and give me a copy of this letter to indicate that you agree in principle to buy my property as explained above. I will then be able to withdraw the property from the market.

[THE FOLLOWING PARAGRAPH APPLIES ONLY IF AN ESTATE AGENT IS **NOT** INVOLVED]:

As no estate agent is involved in this transaction, this letter takes the place of the *memorandum of sale*. Please sign the declaration below and give me a copy of this letter to indicate that you agree in principle to buy my property as explained above. I will then be able to withdraw the property from the market.

If anything is not clear please contact me at any time.

Yours sincerely,

(enter Seller's name)

DECLARATION BY BUYER: I agree in principle to BUY your property on the terms described above, subject to valuation and subject to contract.

Signed: ....Date: ....

Print Name: ....

You should give the Buyer two copies of the above letter so that one copy can be signed and returned to you. You should then help the Buyer further by giving him a draft letter for sending to his solicitor. Here is the wording:

Letter from Buyer to Buyer's solicitor

Dear (Solicitor)

Property: (Address)

I have asked you to act for me in the purchase of a property. I am now writing to explain that I wish to buy the above named property and the details are as follows:

1. Name of Seller: (enter name).

2. Seller's solicitor: (enter name, address, and telephone number).

3. Price for buying property: (enter SELLING PRICE, not discounted amount).

4. Cash Incentive: I have also agreed to receive a Cash Incentive of £ (enter amount). This sum of money is to be paid to me upon completion, from the mortgage amount that I will be borrowing.

I confirm that I will declare the cash incentive on my mortgage application form. (Delete this paragraph if Buyer is not using a loan to buy the property.)

Please find enclosed a copy of a price confirmation letter I have received from the Seller.

Yours sincerely

(name of Buyer)

The above letter from the Buyer to his solicitor is important as it will focus the Buyer's mind into taking the correct action and being committed to following the strategy.

If the Buyer will not sign the declaration in the letter there and then, you should allow the Buyer to take the letter away, and consult their solicitor should they wish to. In this event, you should make it clear that you cannot take the property off the market until the letter is signed or until you get a clear indication of an intention to buy.

Important Note: *When mentioning this strategy to a solicitor, only talk in terms of giving a Cash Incentive to the Buyer. Do not talk in terms of giving a cashback that is deducted from the Buyer's mortgage money, as this is not the case, and solicitors may regard this as somewhat dubious. Also, point out that the Buyer will be declaring the cash incentive on the mortgage application form, and that this is no different to the Cash Incentives given by house-building companies, a practice that is common all over the UK.*

The Valuation Strategy For Sellers then, is using the *Lender's money* rather than the Buyer's own savings to pay for any price gap, for **stamp duty** and other costs. From the Buyer's point of view, in the above example, it is much better to end up with a mortgage of £226,100 and have £10,000 cash in hand, than to end up with a mortgage of £216,600 and no cash in hand.

The Buyer may end up paying a little more in monthly interest on a mortgage of £226,100 compared to £216,600, but the difference is negligible. For example, if the mortgage interest is, say, 5% the monthly payment would be about £942 compared to £903 (a difference of about £39). And remember, the Buyer doesn't have to spend all of the Cash Incentive – he can, if he wants, put some of the Cash Incentive money into a high-interest savings account to offset the small increase in monthly interest.

Or, if the Buyer wanted to, he could use any money remaining from the Cash Incentive to reduce his mortgage. He could even factor the Cash Incentive into the mortgage deposit, thus reducing the amount he has to pay as a deposit. The main advantage is of course the fact that he has £10,000 cash in hand (in this example) at a time when he most likely needs it.

If a Buyer is buying a home with limited savings and limited income, a Cash Incentive can sometimes make or break a property deal. But do not let the Buyer get confused between a 'Cash Incentive' and a 'mortgage cashback'. The 'Cash Incentive' is what you, the Seller, offers him; the 'mortgage cashback' is completely different and is offered by the mortgage company. Of course, there is nothing to stop a Buyer getting both kinds of cashbacks in the same deal.

The Big Question

We now come to the question: *How do you get a full market valuation?* In the above example we need to get a valuation of £238,000 for this strategy to work. If the valuation carried out by the Lender is different to the PRICE what will happen?

If the VALUATION is *less than the PRICE*, the Lender will either say NO to the LOAN, or offer a reduced LOAN based on the lower VALUATION.

If the VALUATION is the *same as or higher than the PRICE*, the Lender will grant the LOAN applied for. Note that normally the Valuer will try to make the valuation match the PRICE, knowing that both the Lender and the Buyer want this.

When the Buyer applies for a mortgage he will be stating the PRICE on the application form, e.g. £238,000. The Lender then instructs a local estate agent or valuation company to carry out a valuation. Note that although the Buyer is paying for the valuation, the Valuer is working for the Lender and reports back to the Lender.

For this strategy to work, then, it is essential to get as high a valuation as possible, and not lower than the proposed PRICE. So how do you make sure that the Buyer gets the VALUATION that he needs for his mortgage? This is how:

Step one: check out local property prices

- Before offering the property for sale find out the approximate values of similar properties in the area. Do this by enquiring at local estate agents, by checking local property newspapers and by walking or driving around the area looking for other properties for sale or sold. This is the beginning of your research to find COMPARABLES.

- If this initial research reveals several more highly priced properties that could be COMPARABLES, you know you may be able to apply *The Valuation Strategy For Sellers*. If you find that there are no similar properties at higher prices, or that the property you want to sell is not undervalued, you should consider not applying *The Valuation Strategy For Sellers*. If you find that comparable prices are *lower* rather than higher, you may have to reconsider the selling price or apply *The Price Strategy For Sellers* instead. Either way, your time will not be wasted.

Step two: Use the Internet to get comparables

- Get property prices for the particular postcode by using the Internet. Simply go to **http://www.landreg.gov.uk/propertyprice/interactive/ppr_u albs.asp**. Then enter a postcode and you will immediately get details of the average price of different types of properties.

For example, if you are selling a flat in postcode RG1 7NT, you will see that in the last three months 43 flats were sold in this postcode, and the average price was £149,881. This is a **free service**. You can also get this information by phone or email but you will be charged £10 (Telephone 0151 473 6008, **Email** enquiries.pic@landregistry.gov.uk).

Why is this information useful? Because if prices for similar properties are higher you know you will be able to find some good comparables. If prices for similar properties are lower, you may have to reconsider *The Valuation Strategy For Sellers*. Instead, you could apply *The Price Strategy For Sellers* (should you get a lower offer to buy your property than you can accept).

- Get comparables from *Home Track* on the Internet. Go to **http://www.hometrack.co.uk** (Tel 0800 019 4440) where you will be able to get a detailed market report for properties in any given postcode. The cost is about £15, and for that you get in-depth analysis of property, prices and trends, all focused on a particular postcode. You also get a list of local comparables and their locations, shown by dots on a street map. So although you don't get the actual addresses of comparables, there is enough information for you to be able to go there and see the property and the address. Naturally, you should be focused on the comparables with the highest values, and begin to compile a shortlist for giving to the Valuer.

- Once you have a few comparables, you may want to know the details of specific comparables. For instance, you may want to know the name of the owner, the actual price paid, the name of the Lender, and so on. To get this kind of information you can either knock on the front door and make enquiries, or you can get most of this information from the Land Registry. For a fee of just £2 you can get a copy of the Land Registry Entry *for any given property* in the UK, showing the legal history, price, date sold, full names of owners, etc. You can do this online over the internet by going to: **www.landregisteronline.gov.uk** and following the prompts to buy online.

Alternatively contact the Land Registry:
Telephone 0151 4736008
Fax 0151 4710151
Email: ***enquiries.pic@landregistry.gov.uk***.

This is worth doing for the shortlist of two or three comparables that you will be giving to the Valuer – by giving the Valuer the full works (i.e. copies of the Land Registry entries) he won't have to double check the veracity of the information and he will be more inclined to go by the prices you give him.

Step three: Meet Valuer at property

- Clearly if you are selling your home *you* are likely to be the person to meet the Valuer. In any event it is important to make sure that you arrange to meet the Valuer at the property when he goes along to do the valuation. *This is critical. There is no other way of giving him the comparables.* Do this by telling the Buyer to state on his mortgage application form that the Valuer *must make an appointment with you, the Seller,* to gain access to the property. Then, when the Valuer contacts you to make an appointment, agree a date and time and make sure there will be no problems with the house occupants and gaining access on the day.

- Meet the Valuer at the property (be polite and friendly). Walk around with the Valuer, and offer to help in any way.

- Give the Valuer the comparables that you have prepared beforehand, and say *'to help you save time I have obtained some comparables which you can take with you'.* Remember two things: (i) The Valuer is working for the Buyer's *Lender,* and (ii) he will use the PRICE given to him *by the Lender and by you* as a guide for arriving at a valuation figure. The Valuer will be trying hard to give a value that is *equal* to the PRICE rather than some other figure, provided the COMPARABLES stack up.

Summary of *The Valuation Strategy For Sellers:*

1. Brief your solicitor about the use of a *'Cash Incentive'* to sell your property. Say that you will be asking the Buyer to accept a small Cash Incentive. By all means explain the strategy to the Solicitor, but you should not need to. If the solicitor is not familiar with the concept of a Cash Incentive find another solicitor. The purpose here is to 'prime' your solicitor to be receptive and to fully co-operate with the Buyer's solicitor when the time comes. Any experienced conveyancer will be familiar with the concept of a Cash Incentive.

2. Prepare a list of local COMPARABLES so that you can be ready to apply *The Valuation Strategy For Sellers* should it be necessary. Use the highest valued comparables in the area by doing research in the locality and on the Internet, and prepare a shortlist of three.

3. Get full Land Registry copies of the selected COMPARABLES (the current cost is £2 each over the Internet) if you will be giving them to the Valuer.

4. Prepare copies of advertisements used by national building companies showing Cash Incentives and explain to the Buyer that what you are proposing is no different.

5. Prepare the Buyer Benefits sheet to help Buyer understand the strategy.

6. Use this strategy only if the Buyer is not able or willing to pay the minimum SELLING PRICE you require. Then apply *The Valuation Strategy For Sellers* exactly as explained in this chapter, taking care to ensure that the Buyer understands how the Cash Incentive works. Reassure the Buyer that this is a perfectly legal and common way of doing business.

7. Before finishing the negotiations, tell the Buyer the next step is to inform his solicitor (and estate agent if applicable). Do this by using the sample letters given above.

8. Tell Buyer to enter the agreed full market value as the SELLING PRICE on the mortgage application form, and clearly state that the Valuer must contact you, the Seller, personally to arrange to see the property for the VALUATION (no alternative contacts must be given to the Valuer). It is crucial that you are able to meet the Valuer at the property because this is the only opportunity you have if you are going to give him the COMPARABLES.

9. Follow through with all parties (Buyer, Estate Agent, and Solicitor) to get things moving.

Stamp Duty Avoidance Strategy No. 6:

The Combination Strategy For Sellers

So far we have looked at the following five strategies:

1	The Tax Exemption Strategy For Sellers
2	The Threshold Strategy For Sellers
3	The Link Strategy For Sellers
4	The Price Strategy For Sellers
5	The Valuation Strategy For Sellers

The Combination Strategy For Sellers is a way of exploiting any 'mix and match' of these five strategies to give a powerful and infallible way of avoiding or reducing the cost of stamp duty as a way of attracting buyer interest, achieving a successful sale, and getting a good price.

Every time you sell a property you will be using a different mix of these strategies, depending on the circumstances. Furthermore, it is unlikely that you will be using just one of these strategies whenever selling a property.

So let's look at how you can combine these strategies to make the property sale as successful as possible. Clearly, you need to understand the five preceding strategies by studying this book, before continuing with this chapter.

The Tax Exemption Strategy For Sellers, based on getting tax relief in disadvantaged areas, is a clear cut situation: it either applies or does not apply. If it does apply, then it would be used in conjunction with other strategies in this book.

The Threshold Strategy For Sellers, based on exploiting stamp duty thresholds, should always be considered if the asking PRICE is near to or within the price threshold. For example, if you think your property is worth about £250,000, you need to price it at less than £251,000 or more than £260,000 to attract interest.

If offering the property at a price between £250,000 and £270,000, it should ideally be offered free of stamp duty, and if you don't get the asking price you could apply *The Price Strategy For Sellers* or *The Valuation Strategy For Sellers.*

The Link Strategy For Sellers, based on avoiding a punitive rate of stamp duty when buying more than one property from the same Seller, can be combined with just about any other strategy in this book. You would, of course, only consider using this strategy if there was a possibility of selling a property to a Buyer that has already bought a property from you in the past (or if selling two or more properties to anybody).

As *The Link Strategy For Sellers* advocates selling one property at a time (if selling to the same person) it can easily be combined, for example, with *The Valuation Strategy For Sellers* if you do not get the asking price. There are endless combinations, depending on particular circumstances.

The point is this: whatever property deal you may be orchestrating, exploit any and all of the strategies in whichever ways are possible. Some property deals may warrant all the strategies! Others may just warrant one of the strategies. Most property deals will be amenable to at least two of the strategies. It would be very unusual to sell a property without being able to apply at least one of the stamp-duty-avoidance strategies in this book.

We now come to the ideal *combination strategy method* that gives a virtually foolproof way of saving money to pay for stamp duty (see Fig. 7 on next page).

FIG. 7 - COMBINATION STRATEGY METHOD

The Valuation Strategy For Sellers	This strategy is based on the Seller giving a Cash Incentive that is related to the VALUATION of the property, and will apply whenever prices of comparable properties are higher. **Use this strategy when asking price not accepted or when there is a price gap to overcome *and* prices of COMPARABLES are higher** (If price is the same or lower, use *The Price Strategy For Sellers*)
The Price Strategy For Sellers	This strategy is based on the Seller giving a Cash Incentive that is equivalent to the price reduction the Seller is willing to give, and will apply whenever *The Valuation Strategy For Sellers* cannot be used. **Use this strategy when asking price not accepted or when there is a price gap to overcome *and* prices of COMPARABLES are the same or lower.** (If price is higher, use *The Valuation Strategy For Sellers*)

Fig. 7 shows when to use these strategies, so that *whatever the comparables* we still have a viable strategy for proposing to a potential Buyer. If the comparables are higher than the proposed selling price use ***The Valuation Strategy For Sellers***. If comparables are the same or lower, use ***The Price Strategy For Sellers***. In both instances we assume that a price has been negotiated but not agreed because there is a price gap that needs bridging.

These are strategies for keeping 'up your sleeve' should it not be possible to agree a selling price. When a Seller is thinking of selling a property he should first check the local comparables.

176

Then, depending on how the local prices compare, he would decide whether to have *The Valuation Strategy For Sellers* in reserve or *The Price Strategy For Sellers* in reserve.

Combining these two strategies is at the heart of stamp duty avoidance, and to fully appreciate how this works several examples follow. Study these examples carefully as they show how the strategy works in practice.

Example 1.

1. Asking price for apartment is £150,000.

2. Price is negotiated down to £148,000 but it is not enough to satisfy the Buyer.

3. Using *The Price Strategy For Sellers* you could offer the Buyer a £2,000 Cash Incentive (so Seller would get £148,000 and Buyer would get a £2,000 Cash Incentive). But prior to negotiating the deal you checked the COMPARABLES and established that the best similar apartments nearby have sold at about £155,000.

4. Since the COMPARABLES are higher than your asking price of £150,000 you decide to use *The Valuation Strategy For Sellers*. So you offer the Buyer a £7,000 Cash Incentive. Note that £7,000 is the total of the price reduction (£2,000) and the COMPARABLES (on average £5,000 higher). So Seller gets £148,000 and Buyer gets a £7,000 Cash Incentive. The selling price would be registered at £155,000. This is how you *combine* the two strategies.

5. If the COMPARABLES had been about the same or lower than the asking price, you would have used *The Price Strategy For Sellers* and just asked offered a £2,000 Cash Incentive.

6. Naturally, you would also use any of the other strategies that may apply.

Example 2.

1. Asking price for apartment is £150,000.

2. Price is negotiated down to £146,000 but it is not enough to satisfy the Buyer.

3. Using **The Price Strategy For Sellers** you could offer the Buyer a £4,000 Cash Incentive (so Seller would get £146,000 and Buyer would get a £4,000 Cash Incentive). But prior to negotiating the deal you checked the COMPARABLES and established that the best similar apartments nearby have sold at about £150,000.

4. Since the COMPARABLES are similar to the <u>asking price</u> of £150,000 you decide to use **The Price Strategy For Sellers**. So you offer the Buyer a £4,000 Cash Incentive. Note that no Cash Incentive for the COMPARABLES can be realized because they are similar in price to the property you are selling. The selling price is registered at £150,000.

5. If the COMPARABLES had been higher than your proposed selling price, you would have used **The Valuation Strategy For Sellers**.

6. Naturally, you would also use any of the other strategies that may apply.

Example 3.

1. Asking price for apartment is £150,000.

2. Price is negotiated down to £149,500. Although this price reduction is small, the Seller simply does not want to reduce it any further. Unfortunately it is not enough to satisfy the Buyer.

3. The COMPARABLES are similar in price.

4. However, the house has a conservatory, whereas the three COMPARABLES that have been shortlisted do not have conservatories. This is a 'unique feature' and it puts the value of your property up by £3,000 in relation to the comparables (remember that you must point this out to the Valuer when you meet him).

5. Note that if your property had, for example, a bigger garden than the COMPARABLES the same principles apply. *Anything* that increases the value of your property (compared to the COMPARABLES) can be used to increase the valuation – the higher the valuation, the bigger the Cash Incentive.

6. Using **The Valuation Strategy For Sellers** you agree a selling PRICE of £153,000 with a Cash Incentive of £3,500, giving the

Seller a net amount of £149,500. Note that the £3,500 Cash Incentive is the total of the price reduction (£500) and the price difference of £3,000 (COMPARABLES at £150,000 and the target property plus conservatory at £153,000). The selling price would be registered at £153,000.

7. In this example you have combined *The Price Strategy For Sellers* and *The Valuation Strategy For Sellers* to give the Buyer a Cash Incentive of £3,500. But note that you would only ever present one of these strategies to the Buyer (otherwise everybody gets confused!). Also, note that as soon as you realized you could use the conservatory to get a higher valuation, you knew that you would only be presenting *The Valuation Strategy For Sellers* to the Buyer.

8. Naturally, you would also use any of the other strategies that may apply.

Example 4.

1. Asking price for apartment is £150,000.

2. A big price reduction is negotiated down to £145,000 (as the kitchen needs modernizing) but it is not enough to satisfy the Buyer, who only wants to pay £140,000.

3. The COMPARABLES are similar in price.

4. The house has a converted second toilet under the stairs, so you check the COMPARABLES and discover the following:

    a. COMPARABLE one has no second toilet and was sold for 149,000.

    b. COMPARABLE two has no second toilet and was sold for £148,000.

    c. COMPARABLE three has a second toilet and was sold for £152,000.

5. You decide to use all three COMPARABLES and you will tell the Valuer that as your property *has a converted second toilet* the value is about £152,000 (same as COMPARABLE 'C').

6. You know straightaway that you will only be using *The Valuation Strategy For Sellers* to bridge the price gap with the Buyer because you are going for a valuation that is greater than your asking price of £150,000. So you will be agreeing a PRICE

of £152,000 with a Cash Incentive of £7,000. Note that £7,000 is the total of the price reduction (£5,000) and the valuation price difference of £2,000 (the COMPARABLE with the second toilet is on average £2,000 higher than the asking price of £150,000).

7. In this example you have combined *The Price Strategy For Sellers* and *The Valuation Strategy For Sellers* to offer a £7,000 Cash Incentive to bridge a price gap of £5,000. But note that you would only ever present one of these strategies to the Buyer (otherwise everybody gets confused!). Also, note that as soon as you realized you could use the converted toilet to get a higher valuation, you knew that you would be presenting *The Valuation Strategy For Sellers* to the Buyer, even though the price reduction was *greater* than the valuation difference.

8. Naturally, you would also use any of the other strategies that may apply.

Example 5.

1. The Seller offers to sell his house at £230,000 plus a £4,000 Cash Incentive. This means the Buyer gets £4,000 on completion which he can use to pay for stamp duty, legal fees, deposit or anything else. The Seller would get a net £226,000 which is the minimum amount acceptable.

2. A Buyer is able to get a 95% mortgage but has little money for the 5% deposit. So the Buyer offers £225,000 but still wants the same £4,000 Cash Incentive.

3. The Seller says this would give him a net £221,000 which is not enough, and the minimum he can accept is £226,000. So the Seller offers the Buyer a solution based on a £9,000 Cash Incentive (see column C in Fig. 8 on the next page).

FIG. 8 - CASH INCENTIVE OFFER

(Example 5)

	A (£) Advertised offer	B (£) Buyer's offer	C (£) Seller's proposal
Selling price	230,000	225,000	235,000
Cash Incentive	4,000	4,000	9,000
Net amount received by seller	226,000	221,000	226,000
Buyer's loan based on 95% mortgage	218,500	213,750	223,250
Buyer's deposit based on 5%	11,500	11,250	11,750
Less Cash Incentive	4,000	4,000	9,000
Amount required for deposit	7,500	7,250	2,750

Column A is the original price advertised by the Seller. Column B is the offer made by the Buyer which cannot be accepted as the Seller wants a minimum of £226,000. Column C is the counter-offer made by the Seller to secure a sale.

The Buyer offered a lower price (£225,000) in the hope of reducing the amount required for his deposit - this is the 'conventional' approach made by most people. Fig. 8 shows that paying £5,000 less (col. B) will only reduce the deposit by £250, an insignificant amount!

The Seller is keen to sell the house so he uses *The Valuation Strategy For Sellers* to agree a SELLING PRICE of £235,000, and he combines this with *The Discount Strategy For Sellers* to give a big Cash Incentive of £9,000.

In example 5 the Seller is happy as he gets the minimum of £226,000 he wanted. The Buyer is happy as he did not lose the house and only had to pay £2,750 deposit instead of £11,750. Of course, against this the Buyer has a slightly bigger mortgage to pay off. But the extra interest is very small compared to the advantages of gaining a valuable property asset, paying a much smaller deposit, and not losing the property to another buyer.

This solution has saved the Buyer much more than the cost of stamp duty and it has enabled the Seller to get a successful sale. Even the tax authorities are happy as they get paid stamp duty on a higher SELLING PRICE. Everybody wins!

Summary of *The Combination Strategy For Sellers*:

1. Study all the strategies for avoiding stamp duty and use those that best apply to your particular property deal.

2. Offer the property 'free of stamp duty' or 'stamp duty paid' as a way of getting a better market response. Also consider offering a Cash Incentive alongside the asking price.

3. Do your homework before putting the property up for sale: check out the COMPARABLES to decide whether to use *The Price Strategy For Sellers* or *The Valuation Strategy For Sellers*. Remember to combine these two strategies, but present only one of these strategies when negotiating.

4. Use high-priced COMPARABLES and/or unique property features to help get a high valuation from the Valuer.

5. Offer the Buyer as big a Cash Incentive as possible (ideally about 5% of the selling price, but not more than 10%) as a way of getting a sale and a good price.

PART THREE

Other Stamp Duty Avoidance Strategies including commercial property

Introduction

This part of the book covers stamp duty avoidance strategies for property Buyers *and* Sellers. The first three strategies apply to residential and non-residential property. Strategy number four onwards is mainly focused on non-residential property such as land and commercial property.

The reader is urged to study either PART 1 or PART 2 of this book before proceeding any further, as this will aid comprehension when reading this section.

Fig. 1 shows a list of the strategies that follow:

FIG. 1 - THE LIST OF STRATEGIES

1	The Gift Strategy
2	The Company Strategy
3	The Back-to-Back Strategy
4	The Threshold Strategy For Non-Residential Property
5	The Link Strategy For Non-Residential Property
6	The Land Strategy For Non-Residential Property
7	The Price Strategy For Non-Residential Property
8	The Valuation Strategy For Non-Residential Property
9	The Combination Strategy For Non-Residential Property

1. THE GIFT STRATEGY

When you buy a property you pay stamp duty. But when you receive a property as a gift stamp duty does not usually apply.

It would be illegal to make a property gift and then receive a hidden, secret or indirect payment for the property without paying stamp duty. Gifting a property to anybody is perfectly legal provided that if and when payment is received, the appropriate stamp duty is paid.

However, there are circumstances when stamp duty can be legally avoided by making use of the gift exemption, so let's look at the possibilities.

Stamp duty is only payable when there is a transfer of ownership *and when* a payment is made for the property. But what is the situation when there is a transfer of ownership and no payment is made?

Answer: No stamp duty is liable. So if John makes a gift of a house to Mary, neither party has to pay stamp duty, regardless of the value of the house and regardless of the relationship between the two people.

The tax authorities do not care whether the gift is between close family members or between strangers, it makes no difference. But they do care about *reciprocity: there must be no reciprocal payment*. The gift must be genuine in the sense that there must be no 'consideration'. That is, there must be no financial payment or payment in kind.

But suppose two people give a property to each other as a gift, i.e. they swap or exchange properties. Do they both pay stamp duty? The answer is YES because the tax authorities do not recognize the verb *swap* or *exchange* when it comes to stamp duty. When you exchange properties you are buying a property from each other (instead of paying money, you are using your property to make a payment in kind).

Here are some examples of what you can and cannot do when it comes to gifts, and how you can avoid stamp duty by using *The Gift Strategy*.

Example 1.

John owns a house worth £270,000. Peter owns a bungalow worth £200,000. They want to exchange properties. If they exchange properties at these prices Peter will have to pay John £70,000 (the price difference between the two properties).

The deal goes ahead, and Peter has to pay stamp duty based on 3% of £270,000 (£8,100). John has to pay stamp duty based on 1% of £200,000 (£2,000). Total stamp duty: £10,100.

Alternative scenario for example 1:

John and Peter may have *thought* about swapping properties and about various pricing possibilities but nothing has been agreed or put in writing (so the *selling prices have not yet been established*). Thus there is no collusion, and after all, they are free to think whatever they like!

Peter and John each decide to advertise their houses for sale at £250,000 and £180,000. They do this in their own separate ways, at different times. This is perfectly legitimate. Among the responses that Peter gets, he decides to contact John. Among the responses that John gets he decides to contact Peter.

Peter decides to accept the advertised offer from John. Later John decides to accept the advertised offer from Peter. John decides to sell his house to Peter for £250,000. And Peter decides to sell his house to John for £180,000. Note that no prices have been *reduced* as a way of avoiding stamp duty – this would be illegal.

The deal goes ahead, and Peter has to pay stamp duty based on 1% of £250,000 (£2,500). John has to pay stamp duty based on 1% of £180,000 (£1,800). Total stamp duty: £4,300 (a big saving of £5,800 compared to the previous scenario!).

In this example three points come to mind:

1. It is perfectly legal to sell a property at any price you like. You can, if you like, sell a house for just £10 and the Buyer would pay no stamp duty. However, *there must be no reciprocity*, i.e. no additional cash payment or payment in kind. If there is a reciprocal payment then stamp duty will apply on the total consideration paid or on the open market value of the property.

2. In the above alternative scenario note that no price reductions were made by either party. John has not reduced the price of his house from £270,000 to £250,000 as a way of avoiding stamp duty (this would be illegal). There are no records to show that John (or his estate agent) has advertised the house for £270,000, and therefore nobody (including the tax authorities) can say that John has reduced the price to £250,000. Equally, there are no records to show that Peter has reduced his price from £200,000 to £180,000. Hence, there has been no reciprocity – just two separate property purchase transactions. In this example, John and Peter were careful to keep separate each property transaction and not making any reference to *swapping* or *exchange*.

3. The key here is to not be accused of swapping properties at a lower market value as a way of avoiding stamp duty. Since no selling price was set and then discounted, there can be no accusations. And providing there is no reciprocity or undeclared payment, the market value of each property becomes irrelevant.

Example 2.

Mother buys a flat in her own name and then gives it to her daughter as a gift. Stamp duty applies when flat purchased by mother. But when the flat is given to daughter as a *gift* no stamp duty applies because there was no consideration.

Example 3.

Mother gives money to daughter as a gift and daughter buys flat in her own name. Stamp duty applies when daughter purchased flat.

Example 4.

John gives his house to Mary as a gift. No stamp duty applies as there was no consideration. A few months later, Mary buys British Airways shares worth £200,000 and gives them as a Christmas present to John. This would be regarded as a payment in kind and stamp duty would be liable on £200,000.

Example 5.

John wants to sell his house to Mary. The market value is £270,000. John decides to sell the house to Mary for £250,000 as a way of reducing stamp duty from 3% to 1%. This is perfectly legal as stamp duty is paid on the *price* regardless of market value. John has in effect given Mary a gift of £20,000 in equity (the difference between £270,000 and £250,000). Should Mary later give John a new car, a financial gift or a payment in kind worth about £20,000, Mary would need to declare the gift to the tax authorities and offer to pay the stamp duty that would be due. In this example Mary would have to pay £5,600 in stamp duty (the difference between 3% of £270,000 and 1% of £250,000).

Example 6.

Father buys house for £190,000 *in his name* and gives it as a gift to his son. Father paid stamp duty (**first stamp duty payment**) when house purchased. Son paid no stamp duty when house received as a gift. Two years later (or two months later) the son mortgages the house and gives £190,000 to father. This must be declared to the tax authorities, as stamp duty would be liable (**second stamp duty payment**) on the payment of £190,000 to father. In this example, stamp duty has been paid twice. This can be avoided as follows: Instead of buying a house in his name, the father can buy the house in *his son's name* and pay stamp duty only once. Then at any time later, the son can mortgage the house and repay the father without any further stamp duty costs.

Example 7.

Angela owns a house with a market value of £240,000 and a mortgage of £150,000. She gives the house as a gift to Robert provided Robert takes over the mortgage. Robert must pay stamp duty on £150,000 even though the house was a gift because the outstanding mortgage is deemed to be a financial payment. Note that if at a future date Robert gives Angela any kind of reciprocal payment for the house gift, there will be a further stamp duty payment to make. Taking over any kind of outstanding mortgage is deemed to be a consideration.

Example 8.

Angela owns a house with a market value of £240,000 and a mortgage of £150,000. She sells her house to Robert for £90,000 on condition he takes over the mortgage. Robert has to pay stamp duty on the total of £150,000 plus £90,000. A property mortgage cannot be 'gifted' as a way of avoiding stamp duty.

These examples show that stamp duty can sometimes be avoided by gifting in legitimate ways that are fully sanctioned by the tax authorities.

It's also important to understand the capital gains tax consequences of gifting property. Detailed information is contained in the Taxcafe guide *How to Avoid Property Tax.*

Another important point relates to 'connected persons' and this is explained through the example that follows.

Example of connected person

- John bought a shop (or house) in his company's name and paid the usual stamp duty. So now John owns the Company that owns the shop. Later, John instructs his Company to give the shop to himself as a gift, i.e. he transfers the shop from his Company's name into his own name. No consideration has been paid as it is a gift.

- As John is 'connected' to the Company that made the gift, he must pay stamp duty upon receiving the gift, based on the open market value of the property. If John's Company had made the gift to a person not connected with the Company, no stamp duty would be payable. The tax authorities regard a person as being 'connected' to a Company if he works for the Company or is a director. The immediate family or close relatives of the connected person are also deemed to be 'connected'.

- The same 'connected person' criterion applies if gifting occurs between connected Companies. Remember that gifting between family members and close relatives is fine and no stamp duty applies provided that no Company is involved.

For a full definition of a 'connected person' see the *'Income and Corporation Taxes Act 1988, section 839'.* You can get a free copy on the internet by going to:
http://www.hmso.gov.uk/acts/acts1988/Ukpga_19880001_en_71.htm#mdiv839.

The Act does not prohibit gifting between connected persons – the purpose of the Act is to collect tax should such gifting occur. Thus, if a property gift is made between connected parties, stamp duty will be applied, based on the open market value. The purpose here is to prevent property transfers within a business group as a way of avoiding tax.

Here is a summary of the things to watch out for when making a property gift (residential or non-residential):

1. No stamp duty applies if the gift is between private individuals. This is so regardless of the relationship between the individuals. It does not matter whether the gift is between family members, spouses, or strangers. The tax authorities are not in the business of judging the nature of human relationships.

2. When a gift is made there must be no reciprocal payment in cash or in kind, otherwise stamp duty will apply.

3. Gifts between Companies, or between a Company and an individual will not attract stamp duty provided there is no connection between the parties. Parties are 'connected' if they are family members or close relatives, or if a person has common interests with both parties.

4. If a property with a mortgage is gifted, the person taking over the mortgage must pay stamp duty on the value of that mortgage.

2. THE COMPANY STRATEGY

This strategy allows you to sell a residential or non-residential property of any value (and in any part of the UK) without any *Stamp Duty Land Tax* being paid to the tax authorities. And naturally, it is completely sanctioned and approved by Inland Revenue. Furthermore, the amount of stamp duty avoided can then be shared in any proportion desired, between Buyer and Seller.

The Company Strategy is based on the following principle:

When you *buy* a property you normally pay stamp duty at the applicable rate. Also, when you *sell* a property, the next Buyer will normally pay stamp duty at the applicable rate. This means *stamp duty is paid twice*: once on the purchase and once on the sale. *The Company Strategy* shows how *stamp duty is only paid once instead of twice!* In other words, stamp duty is paid on the purchase, but not on the sale.

This is how it works:

- John (the Buyer) will form a Company just for the purpose of buying a property. Having formed the Company, John will then buy a property and pay the proper stamp duty in the usual way. So John now owns a Company, and the Company owns a property.

- At some future date, when the property is offered for sale, John becomes the Seller. So the property is now offered for sale in the usual way. But John has a big card up his sleeve. He can offer the property 'stamp duty paid' with virtually no financial loss. John can do this because, instead of selling the property, he can sell the Company that owns the property (when you do this virtually no stamp duty applies).

- John sells the Company by selling all the shares in the company to Peter, the new Buyer. The shares were sold to Peter at a total price equivalent to the price of the property. Peter also has to pay stamp duty when he buys the shares, but the rate is only 0.5%. So now Peter owns the Company that owns the property. The net result is that when the property was sold, the stamp duty rate was only 0.5% regardless of price.

- Peter now has the advantage that when he in turn comes to sell the property he has a ready-made Company that owns the property and only 0.5% stamp duty will apply. However, if Peter wishes, he can sell the property in the conventional way, i.e. his Company can sell the *property* to a Buyer instead of selling *shares* to a Buyer (in which case, the usual property stamp duty rate will apply).

At this point you may be thinking that this is too good to be true. And in fact you would be right to think this because there are in fact two catches. And because of these catches we are not making a big song and dance about this strategy. First we will look at the advantages of this strategy, and then the disadvantages.

Advantages

1. You can buy a property and, in effect, 'recover' the stamp duty when you sell it.
2. The cost of stamp duty is reduced to a maximum of 0.5% regardless of property value.
3. The Strategy can be applied to any value property in any part of the UK.
4. It is completely sanctioned and approved by Inland Revenue.
5. It is ideal for property professionals who buy and *sell* properties (not suitable if planning to keep property for long term).

Disadvantages

(Note: There are two catches, as explained below)

1. **The Company formation.** The protagonist (i.e. the person applying the strategy) will be forming a Company exclusively for the ownership of the target property. This will be a non-trading company that owns just one asset, the target property. The cost of forming a company varies between £20 and £200 depending on whether you do it yourself.

2. **The mortgage.** If the protagonist is buying the property with a mortgage, a commercial mortgage will be required because the property is being purchased in the name of a Company. This should not be too much of a problem because commercial mortgages for property purchases are becoming more widely available in the UK.

3. **Catch no. 1 - Legal undertaking.** The Buyer will not be buying the target property. Instead, the Buyer will be buying the Company that owns the target property. In this regard, the Buyer must instruct his solicitor to buy a Company (rather than a property) from the protagonist, and ensure that full unencumbered ownership of the Company is passed on to him, the Buyer. This requires the protagonist to give the Buyer a *watertight legal undertaking* that the Company is unencumbered, has not traded, and has no claims against it, AND that should anybody make a claim against the company arising from a date before the Company was sold, the protagonist will be personally liable. Giving this *legal undertaking* is no problem (and no risk) for the protagonist, but persuading the Buyer to accept the undertaking may be difficult. Also, there may be additional legal fees for arranging the *legal undertaking* as part of the property transaction.

4. **Catch no. 2 – Tax.** When the protagonist comes to selling the property he has two options:

Option 1: Abandon *The Company Strategy* and sell the property in the conventional way. That is, the Buyer would pay the full stamp duty applicable and buy the property from the protagonist's company. The Company would remain under the ownership of the protagonist, but it would now own nothing except the proceeds of sale. The Company would pay corporation tax on the capital gain and distributing the proceeds to the company owner would have additional tax consequences. It is very likely that the company owner would end up paying more in tax than if the property had never been put in a company.

Option 2: Apply *The Company Strategy* and sell the Company shares to the Buyer as a way of transferring ownership of the company and the property to the new owner. Again the capital gains tax consequences would have to be examined carefully by the buyer and the seller (see the

Taxcafe.co.uk guide *Using a Property Company to Save Tax* for more information). From a legal perspective the buyer may be nervous about acquiring a company instead of just a property. For example, he may fear that the company has unpaid bills or other debts which will become his responsibility. Although this issue can be taken care of in the contract governing the sale of the company, many buyers will probably still be reluctant to buy a company instead of a property.

This is not a strategy that we generally recommend, mainly because of the potential tax and legal ramifications.

3. THE BACK-TO-BACK STRATEGY

This strategy is for people who wish to buy a property and sell it on without incurring the cost of stamp duty. It is particularly applicable if buying 'off-plan' i.e. before the property is built, and then selling the property before completion of purchase.

Normally, if you buy a property and then sell it at a later date, the stamp duty paid on purchase cannot be recovered. However, if you buy a property (whether off-plan, new, or not new) there is a way of avoiding stamp duty if you plan to sell it again.

The strategy is based on selling the property before completion of purchase. This is how it works:

Step 1: You find a property *but before you buy it* you ascertain a potential buyer or market for the property in question. For example, you buy a new flat 'off-plan' in a city centre and you are reasonably confident that in several months' time when the property is built you will be able to sell it on. Alternatively, you find a customer who is looking for a specific property – you then find that specific property and make it available to your customer.

Step 2: You buy the property to the extent that you pay a reservation fee or a deposit and you exchange contracts. At this stage you must make sure that you have an 'assignable contract' (i.e. a contract that allows you to sell the property on to another person without any penalties or legal repercussions). This should not be any problem as most property contracts, particularly off-plan purchases, are assignable. You are now 'committed' to buying the property whether or not you can find a customer to sell on to. Note that you have not yet completed the sale, i.e. you have not yet paid the full price.

Step 3: You find a customer who would like to buy the property instead of you. In this scenario you instruct your solicitor to do a 'back-to-back' transaction so that you can sell the property on to your customer without 'completion' on your part. Then, when your customer completes the purchase he will pay the stamp duty in the normal way. You paid no stamp duty at any point.

Back-to-back property deals where A sells to B, and B sells on to C have two advantages for party 'B':

- Stamp duty is avoided.
- Party 'B' is able to buy a property and sell it on without having to finance the transaction.

The tax authorities are quite happy for this kind of transaction to take place, provided that party 'B' does not *substantially perform*. If you *substantially perform* you will be fully liable to pay stamp duty. What does *substantially perform* mean?

According to the tax authorities, *substantially perform* means the following:

If you have *substantially performed* it means that as far as stamp duty is concerned you have completed the purchase and you have to pay stamp duty *even if the completion of purchase has not occurred yet.*

You are deemed to have *substantially performed* if you have done any of the following:

- Paid 90% or more of the property price.
- Taken possession of the property (e.g. have the keys).
- Paid any rent for the property.
- Carried out any works, alterations or renovations to the property.

However, there is no specified time period in the regulations. So provided you do not *substantially perform*, you can take as long as you like between reserving a property (or exchanging contracts) and finding a customer to sell on to. Naturally, you are likely to face time constraints imposed by the Seller, and at some point the completion of purchase would be expected to go ahead.

Clearly, *The Back-To-Back Strategy For Buyers* is a strategy for property entrepreneurs as it carries an element of risk, i.e. the risk that a customer to sell on to at a profit will not be found. Therefore, you would pursue this strategy for the business potential, and the savings in stamp duty would be regarded as incidental.

4. THE THRESHOLD STRATEGY FOR NON-RESIDENTIAL PROPERTY

In PARTS 1 and 2 of this book we saw how you could avoid or minimize stamp duty in two basic ways:

1. By negotiating a better price if the selling price is over but near a stamp duty threshold. For example if the price is £260,000 it is possible that the price has been put up to this figure to 'get away' from the £250,000 threshold (in which case a good reduction could be negotiated). Alternatively, if a Seller has a house or shop worth £260,000 he can offer the property at £250,000 and arrange to sell a list of chattels for £10,000. This makes the property easier to sell and more attractive to a potential buyer as there will be less stamp duty to pay.

2. By fully exploiting 'chattels' (known as 'movables' in Scotland) to get a price reduction below a stamp duty threshold. Study this subject carefully in PART 1 or 2, as it is important to observe the legal niceties if using this strategy.

Regarding non-residential property, there are no differences in strategy except that the tax thresholds are different. Here's a comparison:

FIG. 2 - COMPARISON OF STAMP DUTY THRESHOLDS
(Only the first threshold is different)

Residential	Non-residential
Over £120,000 = 1%	Over £150,000 = 1%
Over £250,000 = 3%	Over £250,000 = 3%
Over £500,000 = 4%	Over £500,000 = 4%

So, for example, for non-residential property (using the same 'Threshold Strategy' as described in PARTS 1 and 2 of this book) you should look carefully at any selling prices between £151,000 and £170,000 to see if there is room for negotiation.

If chattels, equipment, machinery, commercial stock, or any kind of inventory is involved you may have a dilemma between choosing Scenario A or Scenario B:

Scenario A. The Buyer could negotiate a selling price that includes the chattels or commercial inventory. In this case the Lender pays for the chattels, albeit indirectly as strictly speaking commercial property loans are not meant to cover chattels. The advantage here is that the Buyer does not have to find cash to buy the chattels separately. The disadvantage is that if negotiating a price close to a stamp duty threshold the Buyer has less room for manoeuvre. That is, the Buyer will have less flexibility to use chattels as a way of getting the price reduced to a lower threshold.

Scenario B. The Buyer could negotiate a selling price that does not include chattels or commercial inventory. In this case the Lender does not pay for the chattels (instead the Seller does). The advantage here is that the Buyer can negotiate a below-threshold price to minimize stamp duty. The disadvantage is that the Buyer has to find the cash to pay for the chattels.

Naturally, the choice of scenario A or B above is going to depend on the financial resources of the Buyer, the selling price, and the value of the chattels or commercial inventory.

For the Seller, the decision on whether to offer scenario A or B above depends on several factors:

Does the inventory add value to the business or commercial property being sold? If, for example, you are selling a newsagent's as a 'going concern' then clearly the inventory would be included. And there are Lenders who specialize in commercial mortgages that would include the inventory, the business goodwill, and so on.

On the other hand, if selling an office building, an empty shop, or a factory, there may be good reasons for selling the inventory separately to the mutual benefit of both Buyer and Seller.

The point is this: Always look at chattels, equipment and inventory in a non-residential property transaction to see how best to exploit the deal and minimize stamp duty.

5. THE LINK STRATEGY FOR NON-RESIDENTIAL PROPERTY

The *Link Strategies* in PARTS 1 and 2 of this book apply equally to non-residential and commercial property. However, as we saw in the previous strategy, the stamp duty thresholds are different, as shown below.

COMPARISON OF STAMP DUTY THRESHOLDS
(Only the first threshold is different)

Residential	Non-residential
Over £120,000 = 1%	Over £150,000 = 1%
Over £250,000 = 3%	Over £250,000 = 3%
Over £500,000 = 4%	Over £500,000 = 4%

The *Link Strategy* is particularly effective with commercial property. This is because very often a commercial real-estate deal can involve more than one property. So long as each element of the property deal is registered separately at the Land Registry, then each element of property can be purchased (or sold) separately and should avoid linkage. By using suitable time gaps each element of the property deal can be kept separate, and be sold separately to the same person or company (or be bought separately from the same person or company), resulting in substantial savings in stamp duty. However, make sure you get good legal advice before you proceed to ensure that this strategy will work in your personal circumstances.

Clearly, if buying commercial property that includes an element of residential property they cannot be separated out so as to avoid linkage. For example a flat above a shop, a home on a farm, or a live-in pub come to mind. In these situations you cannot split the residential element from the non-residential element as a way of creating two transactions to minimize stamp duty. The linkage for stamp duty purposes will always be there if sold to or bought from the same person or company.

A question that sometimes arises with commercial or residential property is *How do you deal with a portfolio of properties?* That is, how do you buy several properties from the same source without incurring the punitive 'linked transaction' rate of stamp duty? This can arise when a business that owns several properties changes to new ownership, or when a person that owns a portfolio of properties wants to retire and divest himself of his properties.

The answer is to apply *The Link Strategy* as explained in PARTS 1 and 2 of this book. There is little risk: if *The Link Strategy* is not viable for whatever reason, you are back where you started with nothing lost.

6. THE LAND STRATEGY FOR NON-RESIDENTIAL PROPERTY

Land is regarded by the tax authorities as non-residential property. This is so even if the land being purchased is for residential purposes. The fact that you cannot reside on the land at that moment is what counts.

The rates of stamp duty for non-residential property are as follows:

FIG. 3 - RATES OF STAMP DUTY FOR NON-RESIDENTIAL PROPERTY

Property Price	Stamp Duty
Not more than £150,000	0%
More than £150,000 but not more than £250,000	1%
More than £250,000 but not more than £500,000	3%
More than £500,000	4%

So if you are buying a plot of land to build a home, it is regarded as non-residential property and, as a consequence, no stamp duty applies if the price is not over £150,000.

This strategy can be used to avoid stamp duty if buying land or property for building or re-building purposes.

Clearly, this strategy is only suitable if you are contemplating buying a plot of land and building a property (residential or non-residential). One of the biggest problems faced by builders is 'planning permission'. It is not too difficult to buy land, but getting planning permission to build on the land is usually very difficult and sometimes impossible.

The solution is to buy a dilapidated property, a wreck, or an abandoned property as the land will already have 'planning permission' by virtue of the existing building. The existing building can then be demolished and a new building erected. Naturally, fresh planning permission would need to be obtained but it is far more likely to be granted if a building already existed on the site.

Stamp duty can be avoided by not buying a 'property' as such – instead, you buy the 'land' it is standing on. By doing this, you pay no stamp duty up to a threshold of £150,000 (compared with a threshold of £120,000 for residential property). Here's an example:

An old abandoned bungalow is for sale at £140,000. It has a large garden, big enough to build a new house or a block of flats. Instead of buying the bungalow and paying £1,400 in stamp duty, you agree with the owner that you will buy the property as *land* at the same price of £140,000. By doing this you save £1,400 in stamp duty. In this example, it must be made clear to the Buyer's solicitor that the bungalow is *'no longer suitable as a dwelling and will not be used as such.'*

What's the catch? you may ask. Why not always buy a house as land and avoid stamp duty? The catch is that the property being purchased must not be a *'residential property'* or *'must not be*

suitable as a dwelling.' This is how the tax authorities define a so-called *residential property:*

(Extract from the Finance Act 2003)

(a) A building that is used or suitable for use as a dwelling, or is in the process of being constructed or adapted for such use, and

(b) Land that is or forms part of the garden or grounds of a building within paragraph (a) (including any building or structure on such land), or

(c) An interest in or right over land that subsists for the benefit of a building within paragraph (a) or of land within paragraph (b).

What does this definition really mean? It simply means that an old abandoned building that is <u>no longer suitable</u> for use as a dwelling (or for any other meaningful purpose) is not regarded as *residential property.* And that being the case, it can only be regarded as non-residential property, e.g. commercial property.

Should you want to apply *The Land Strategy For Non-residential Property* and you have found a possible target property, the first step would be to get confirmation from your solicitor that the target property can in fact be purchased as a non-residential property. Alternatively, you may wish to explain to the Seller that he can obtain a better price for the property by having it demolished, thus making the land more attractive to buy. A heap of rubble is more likely to pass the test of *non-residential property* than an abandoned wreck!

A final thought on this subject: If you are looking for a plot of land to build on be sure of getting planning permission, it may be worth buying a dilapidated property (and knocking it down) even if you have to pay stamp duty for the privilege.

7. THE PRICE STRATEGY FOR NON-RESIDENTIAL PROPERTY

As explained in PARTS 1 and 2 of this book, *The Price Strategy* is based on the following principle:

A Buyer and a Seller negotiate and agree a price reduction. The price reduction amount is given to the Buyer as a Cash Incentive. The money for the Cash Incentive originates from the Lender, but is paid to the Buyer via the Seller. That is why it is called a 'Cash Incentive'.

If you are not sure how this works please refer to the *Price Strategy* chapters in PARTS 1 or 2 of this book before proceeding.

The Price Strategies described in PARTS 1 and 2 also apply to land and commercial property in just the same way.   The difference, of course, is that the property being bought or sold is classified as non-residential property, e.g. commercial property or land.

Note that if a residential property is being purchased (or sold) in the name of a company stamp duty is paid at the rate applicable to *residential* property.

House building companies in the UK have been using ***The Price Strategies*** described in this book for many years, albeit packaged slightly differently.   Hence, the legality of including a cash incentive in the deal is a well-trodden road.

In applying ***The Price Strategy For Non-residential Property*** the following considerations should be taken into account:

1.   It may not be enough to talk to a 'company representative'. Negotiations will need to be conducted with the true decision maker. If dealing with an estate agent it will be important to get past the agent and reach the decision maker direct. If this is not possible, then negotiations can be conducted through the estate agent provided the agent is in contact with the decision maker.

2.   It does not matter whether a company is buying from a private individual, or a private individual buying from a company, or a company buying from a company. ***The Price Strategy For Non-residential Property*** is valid in all these permutations.

3. Step 3 in *The Price Strategies* (as explained in PARTS 1 and 2 of this book) require two letters to be signed in principle (by the Buyer or Seller) to confirm details and to indicate a willingness to proceed. If the land or commercial property being bought or sold belongs to a business, then any communications from that business should be on the letterhead of the business.

8. THE VALUATION STRATEGY FOR NON-RESIDENTIAL PROPERTY

As explained in PARTS 1 and 2 of this book, *The Valuation Strategy* is based on the following principle:

A Buyer and a Seller negotiate and agree an AMOUNT as payment for the property. Another higher figure is agreed as the SELLING PRICE based on comparable property. The difference between the AMOUNT and the SELLING PRICE is given to the Buyer as a Cash Incentive. The money for the Cash Incentive originates from the Lender, but is paid to the Buyer via the Seller/solicitor.

If you are not sure how this works please refer to the *Valuation Strategy* chapters in PARTS 1 or 2 of this book before proceeding.

The Valuation Strategies described in PARTS 1 and 2 also apply to land and commercial property in just the same way. The difference, of course, is that the property being bought or sold is classified as non-residential property, e.g. commercial property or land.

Note that if a residential property is being purchased (or sold) in the name of a company stamp duty is paid at the rate applicable to *residential* property.

House building companies in the UK have been using *The Valuation Strategies* described in this book for many years, albeit packaged slightly differently. Hence, the legality of including a cash incentive in the deal is a well-trodden road.

In applying *The Valuation Strategy For Non-residential Property* the following considerations should be taken into account:

1. **Direct negotiations.** It may not be enough to talk to a 'company representative'. Negotiations will need to be conducted with the true decision maker. If dealing with an estate agent it will be important to get past the agent and reach the decision maker direct. If this is not possible, then negotiations can be conducted through the estate agent provided the agent is in contact with the decision maker.

2. **Buying in a company name.** It does not matter whether a company is buying from a private individual, or a private individual buying from a company, or a company buying from

a company. *The Valuation Strategy For Non-residential Property* is valid in all these permutations.

3. **Written communications.** Step 3 in *The Price Strategies* (as explained in PARTS 1 and 2 of this book) require two letters to be signed in principle (by the Buyer or Seller) to confirm details and to indicate a willingness to proceed. If the land or commercial property being bought or sold belongs to a business, then any communications from that business should be on the letterhead of the business.

4. **Comparable prices.** Comparables for some types of non-residential property may not be readily available in the locality. The way round this is go further away or use comparables which are not so physically similar. This is how Valuers and Estate Agents arrive at 'open market values' for non-residential property when there is no similar business/property nearby.

5. **The business.** Unlike residential property, non-residential property can sometimes include other things which add value to the total selling price. This can be the case when *a whole business is being sold* (not just the commercial property). For example, business goodwill, equipment and machinery, commercial inventory, trading history, business performance, and so on. When such factors are taken into account in arriving at an overall selling price, a comparable is sometimes not possible to find. However, the market value of, for example, the physical premises will be assessed separately for stamp duty purposes. Therefore a comparable for the *building* is what you are after, not a comparable for the *business*.

6. **Stamp duty assessment.** In assessing stamp duty on a non-residential property transaction, the tax authorities take into account three things: The selling price of the physical property, the fixtures and fittings, and the inherent goodwill. Let's look at each of these in turn.

6.1 Selling price of physical property. Stamp duty is payable on the selling price agreed for the commercial property or land. Very often, when buying commercial property it may be part of a package of other goods and services. It is important, therefore, to separate the non-residential property-element of the contract so that this element is listed and priced separately in the contract.

For example if buying a shop as a going concern, stamp duty is payable on the shop premises, but not the inventory. Another good example is a fish and chip shop: You don't pay stamp duty on the market value of the fryers. So when you buy a business you want to buy a 'shopping list' of separately priced items one of which is the commercial property.

If this cost is not separated out there is a risk that the tax authorities will expect stamp duty to be paid on the whole cost of the business or *on their estimate* of 'the open market value' of the property.

Note that you are only interested in comparables if a mortgage applies and if, as a Buyer, you want a Cash Incentive out of the deal. If you are a Seller, you want to be able to offer a Cash Incentive to a Buyer as a way of securing a sale. The Cash Incentive can be used by the Buyer to pay for stamp duty and other costs that cannot normally be included in the mortgage.

6.2 Fixtures and fittings. Stamp duty is payable on fixtures and fittings (including commercial equipment and machinery *fixed* to or forming a part of the property/land) as they are regarded as 'inherent to the property'. There is no need to list fixtures and fittings separately – you simply include them in the price since there is no financial advantage in separating them. You may however list the fixtures and fittings for the benefit of the Buyer and solicitor to avoid any misunderstandings over what is being sold. Fixtures and fittings cannot be purchased separately as a way of avoiding stamp duty or as a way of getting a price reduction. However, chattels (known as 'movables' in Scotland) *can be* purchased separately as a way of avoiding stamp duty, or as a way of getting a price reduction. Chattels and movables include the following:

- Any kind of goods, stock, office equipment, or commercial inventory so long as they are not physically fixed to the property.

- Any commercial intangibles such as skills, knowledge and expertise; trademarks, brands, and patents; assets such as vehicles and valuables; and any other items of value not physically attached to the property.

6.3 Inherent goodwill. Stamp duty is payable on 'inherent goodwill' but not on 'business goodwill'. The value of inherent goodwill is added to the value of the physical property for assessment purposes.

- **Inherent goodwill** is defined somewhat informally by the tax authorities (as it is a matter of 'interpretation') as being *'goodwill that is inherent to the physical location'* being sold. For example, a pub called 'Shakespeare' sited opposite the house where Shakespeare lived would benefit from custom by virtue of its business name in relation to its physical location (i.e. the customers or goodwill come to it because of its physical location). Another example might be a tourist shop close to Hadrian's Wall that specialized in Hadrian's Wall paraphernalia (the goodwill arises from its physical location). A football clothing shop close to a football stadium, or a boat shop next to a lake might be other examples.

- **Business goodwill** does not attract any stamp duty, and can be defined as an intangible asset valued according to the advantage or reputation a business has acquired (over and above its tangible assets). The way to minimize stamp duty in a commercial transaction is to emphasize 'business goodwill' rather than 'Inherent goodwill' (assuming this to be the case). Clearly, if inherent goodwill applies, then this should be mentioned as applicable.

- Try to keep the value of business goodwill as low as possible, perhaps by increasing the value of other chattels and movables to 'even things out'. That way, if the tax authorities want to argue that the business goodwill should be classified as inherent goodwill, the amount involved will not be so big. If it is clear that inherent goodwill will not apply, realize that business goodwill, chattels, and commercial inventory are factors that can be priced to advantage as a way of minimizing stamp duty.

9. THE COMBINATION STRATEGY FOR NON-RESIDENTIAL PROPERTY

The *Combination Strategies* in PARTS 1 and 2 of this book show how various strategies can be combined to good effect.   In particular *The Price Strategy* and *The Valuation Strategy* go hand in hand and should always be considered together when trading in non-residential property.   If anything, non-residential property gives greater scope than residential property for combining various strategies because of the higher nil-tax threshold (£150,000) and because of a greater variety of chattels and movables that might be available for negotiation.

For example, if buying a car repair shop the price could be negotiated below a tax threshold by offering to buy valuable car repair equipment that is not fixed to the property.   If no such equipment is available, then a price could be paid for the *'Business Goodwill'* (there is no stamp duty on Business Goodwill).   A Cash Incentive equivalent to the price reduction could also obtained. For an even bigger Cash Incentive, the Buyer could try to get a good comparable. The point here is that all the ways of combining the strategies for residential property are equally valid for non-residential property.

Taxcafe Question & Answer Service

Need Affordable & Expert Tax Planning Advice?

Try Our Unique Question & Answer Service

The purpose of this guide is to provide you with detailed guidance on how to pay less Stamp Duty on your property investments.

Ultimately you may want to take further action or obtain advice personal to your circumstances.

Taxcafe.co.uk has a unique online tax advice service that provides access to highly qualified tax professionals at an affordable rate.

No matter how complex your question, we will provide you with detailed tax planning guidance through this service. The cost is just £69.95.

To find out more go to **www.taxcafe.co.uk** and click the Tax Questions button.

Pay Less Tax!

... with help from Taxcafe's unique tax guides and software

All products available online at **www.taxcafe.co.uk**

- ➢ **How to Avoid Property Tax**. Essential reading for property investors who want to know all the tips and tricks to follow to pay less tax on their property profits.

- ➢ **Using a Property Company to Save Tax.** How to massively increase your profits by using a property company... plus all the traps to avoid.

- ➢ **How to Avoid Tax on Your Stock Market Profits**. This guide contains detailed advice on how to pay less capital gains tax, income tax and inheritance tax on your stock market investments and dealings.

- ➢ **How to Avoid Inheritance Tax**. A-Z of Inheritance Tax planning, with clear explanations & numerous examples. Covers simple & sophisticated tax planning.

- ➢ **Non Resident & Offshore Tax Planning**. How to exploit non-resident tax status to reduce your tax bill, plus advice on using offshore trusts and companies.

- ➢ **Incorporate & Save Tax**. Everything you need to know about the tax benefits of using a company to run your business.

- ➢ **Bonus vs Dividend**. Shows how shareholder/directors of companies can save thousands in tax by choosing the optimal mix of bonus and dividends.

- ➢ **Selling a Business.** A potential minefield with numerous traps to avoid but significant tax saving opportunities.

- ➢ **How to Claim Tax Credits.** Even families with higher incomes can make successful tax credit claims. This guide shows how much you can claim and how to go about it.

- ➢ **Property Capital Gains Tax Calculator.** Unique software performs complex Capital Gains Tax calculations in seconds.

Printed in the United Kingdom
by Lightning Source UK Ltd.
105919UKS00001B/229-429